SETTING THE RECORD STRAIGHT

MORMONS
&MASONS

D1468826

SETTING THE RECORD STRAIGHT

MORMONS
&MASONS

Gilbert W. Scharffs, Ph.D.

Millennial Press, Inc.
P.O. Box 1741
Orem, UT 84059

ISBN: 1-932597-37-9

Cover design and typesetting by Adam Riggs

To my family, friends, and students, who have been an inspiration to me.

Contents

Acknowledgments xi

Introduction 1

Joseph Smith and Temple/Masonic Chronology 13

Frequent Charges and Answers 21

   1. Is the claim by critics that Joseph Smith stole the
      LDS temple ceremony from the Masons valid? 21

   2. Since prophets and apostles ended with the Bible,
      how can Latter-day Saints claim their temple
      ceremony came from God? 24

   3. Why did Masons in Illinois turn against Joseph
      Smith if he did not plagiarize their ritual? 25

   4. Since Joseph Smith claimed to restore the Church
      that Christ established, why did he get involved
      with another religion? 26

   5. How did those who were Masons before becoming
      Latter-day Saints react to LDS rituals in Joseph
      Smith's day? 29

   6. What is the relationship between Mormons and
      Masons since Nauvoo? 31

   7. What are some differences between Mormon and
      Masonic rituals? 35

   8. Because secrecy is contrary to Christianity, does
      that not invalidate the LDS temple ceremony? 37

9. Why are signs and symbols necessary in making covenants? 39

10. What is the difference between covenants and signs and symbols? 39

11. Aren't symbols on early Latter-day Saint temples copied from Masonry? 40

12. What have Masons who are also LDS said about the two ceremonies? 42

13. How can Latter-day Saints claim the temple endowment is inspired when there have been changes over the years? 44

14. Since Latter-day Saints claim the LDS temple ceremony is biblical, what are some examples? 45

15. Since the Bible says there is no marriage in heaven, isn't marriage for time and eternity in the LDS temples a false concept? 48

16. Is there any support for LDS temple teachings being found in ancient civilizations? 49

17. Did Joseph Smith give the Masonic distress call just before he was murdered at Carthage? 53

Conclusion **61**

Appendix 1 .... **63**

Appendix 2 .... **67**

1. The temple is a two-for-one bargain that helps individuals overcome selfishness. 67

2. The temple ceremony is an example that repetition is a vital principle of learning and communication skills. 68

3. The temple uses the same teaching method the Savior used. 68

4. The house of the Lord answers the questions that have concerned philosophers, theologians and all other people throughout the ages. 69

5. The house of the Lord reminds us of our eternal heritage. 69

6. Latter-day Saints are fulfilling prophecy when they attend the temple. 69

7. Participation in the house of the Lord requires a high level of worthiness. 70

8. The house of the Lord teaches us the principle of reporting our actions. 70

9. The temple emphasizes that we are responsible to the Lord for our behavior. 70

10. Continual, regular visits to the temple and renewing our covenants with the Lord give us strength to do more than just pay lip service. 71

11. In the house of the Lord the biblical teachings of the nature of God are emphasized. 71

12. The temple emphasizes the true nature of man as the Bible teaches. 71

13. The house of the Lord teaches the biblical principles of man's destiny. 72

14. Marriage that can last into the eternities is performed in the temple. 72

15. Qualifying for a temple marriage increases the chance of finding a wonderful mate. 73

16. A temple marriage promotes real love, because it is based on trust. 73

17. A meaningful love is more likely if both husband and wife are drawing closer to God. 73

18. The house of the Lord is a safeguard against the sin of adultery. 74

19. The house of the Lord elevates women and men to their rightful positions as equally important, but different in the eyes of God. 74

20. Temple-attending parents have the power of example in raising children. 75

21. The house of the Lord gives us a time and a place to meditate. 75

22. Going to the temple fulfills our need to have sacred ritual in our lives. 76

23. Temple participation enables us to become more like Christ the Savior. 76

24. Work in temples on behalf of the dead encourages us to pursue family history. 77

25. Performing ordinances for our own ancestors in the house of the Lord brings extra joy. 78

26. The house of the Lord is available to everyone who chooses to qualify. 79

27. The temple may be the only place in the world where strict observance of biblical commandments is required to enter. 79

28. The temple ceremony gives the correct meaning of the term "chosen people." 79

29. The house of the Lord gives credence to the LDS claim of being God's official church on earth because it makes it possible for all mankind to return to God's presence. 80

Appendix 3 83
Bibliography 89
Author's Biographical Information 91

Acknowledgments

Thanks to my wife, Judy, who gave suggestions, did much of the research for this book, and collected photos. Thanks also to Paul Smith, my colleague at the Institute of Religion and BYU Nauvoo, and to Neil Lambert, another Nauvoo faculty member, who answered many of my questions. Appreciation also goes to my Masonic acquaintance and member of the Church, Greg Kearney, who set me straight when I needed answers. I am also grateful for the information I gathered from previous authors dealing with Mormons and Masonry: Don Colvin, Matthew Brown, Kenneth Godfrey, Milton Backman, Donald Cannon, Reed Durham, Hugh Nibley, Mervin B. Hogan, Michael Griffith, Michael Hickenbotham, Richard Bushman, Glen M. Leonard, John Welch, and others.

This book would not have been possible without the encouragement of Randy Bott and Lindsey Shumway of Millennial Press. And my thanks goes to our children Yvette, Brett, Lisa, and Calvin, who cheered us on.

Introduction

*The Apostle Peter taught, "Be ready to give an answer to every-
one who asketh" (1 Peter 3:15).*

*The Apostle Neal Maxwell in our day said that we need no
longer let others "make uncontested dunks."*[1]

There were boycotts, protests, and discussions everywhere,
it seemed. On the news, magazine cover stories, talk shows,
and in churches the topic was always *The Da Vinci Code*. When
the movie opened it was not only "in a theater near you" but
in many theaters near you. Megaplexes showed it in several
theaters starting every thirty minutes. Following the text of the
Dan Brown book closely, the movie created one of the most
controversial cinema events since Mel Gibson's *The Passion*.

The inside front cover of Brown's book states, "The documents, rituals and organizations are historically accurate,"
which seems to mean it is history. No mention of fiction was
made. Only later when the uproar began did the promoters
start calling it a novel in order to quell the protests.

However, in an ABC television interview in New York,
Dan Brown was asked, "If you were writing it as a nonfiction
book, how would it have been different?" To which he replied,
"I don't think it would have."[2]

The *Da Vinci Code* was actually historical fiction, meaning it

---

1. Scharffs, Gilbert W, *The Missionary's Little Book of Answers* [2002]4.
2. Haag, Michael and Veronica, *The Rough Guide to The Da Vinci Code*
[2004] 16.

1

was partly true and partly fiction. The problem, however, is that few would know which parts were true and which were not.

The book and movie proclaimed that Jesus Christ was a mere mortal, not divine, and was married and had a family.[3] This is offensive to most Christians, especially Catholics, who were also accused of suppressing this information and harboring secret organizations.

It was an exciting movie and helped me to better understand the book. But as I sat there I had feelings of dismay that it was derogatory to my Christian faith, and I felt sorrow for my Catholic friends whose church was portrayed in a most negative way.

Other books, articles, or web sites are coming out regularly that claim to be factual and attack the biblical account of Jesus Christ and put Christianity in a bad light. One of the most famous books in recent times was *Quest for the Historical Jesus*, by Albert Schweitzer. His conclusion: Jesus Christ never existed.

The Church of Jesus Christ of Latter-day Saints absolutely proclaims the divinity of Christ and has much additional evidence besides the Bible. We cherish the Book of Mormon, Another Testament of Jesus Christ.

The LDS Church also receives a constant barrage of false negative attacks. These portrayals often degrade the temple ceremonies, which are most sacred and essential to Latter-day Saints, outlining for them God's plan of happiness for this life and all eternity.

Freemasons (also called Masons), who became heavily involved with the Latter-day Saints in Illinois in the early 1840s,

---

3. Although the LDS Church does not have an official doctrine that Jesus was married, many Latter-day Saints believe it is a possibility. LDS members believe that if evidence or revelation confirms that Jesus was married, it would in no way diminish Christ as being the literal son of God the Father. Mormons also do not believe Mary Magdalene was a prostitute, as *The Da Vinci Code* portrays and some denominations teach.

Joseph Smith (left). Founder of The Church of Jesus Christ of Latter-day Saints. He became a Mason in Nauvoo and authorized a Masonic Hall to be built. Abraham Jonas (right). The Mason who was Grand Master for Illinois, who improperly sanctioned the Nauvoo Lodge.

also have solemn rituals. They, too, have been unfairly portrayed over the years.

A charge that flares up from time to time against the LDS Church is that our temple rituals were stolen from the Masons by Joseph Smith, the first Mormon prophet. He joined the group in Nauvoo, Illinois, on March 15, 1842. On this date a Masonic Lodge that met in a grove of trees was established by Illinois Grand Master Abraham Jonas. A year earlier, on April 6, 1841, a cornerstone was laid in Nauvoo to build another LDS temple.

Previously in that year, on January 19, Joseph Smith received a revelation that included the following: "Let this house be built unto my name that I may reveal mine ordinances therein unto my people; for *I deign to reveal unto my church things which have been kept hid from before the foundation of the world*, things that pertain to the dispensation of the fulness of times. And I will show unto my servant Joseph all things pertaining to this house, and the priesthood thereof" (D&C 124:40–42; emphasis added). The Mormon prophet was thus alerted to receiving, "things which have been kept hid from before the foundation of the world" that pertain to the forthcoming temple.

Joseph Smith was told about a temple where the Lord would appear in latter days, even before the LDS Church was organized in 1830. An angel, by the name of Moroni, appeared to the Prophet and quoted the Savior, saying, "The Lord, whom ye seek, will come suddenly to his temple" (Malachi 3:1; 3 Nephi 24:1; Joseph Smith–History 1:36). Moroni, before he delivered the Book of Mormon plates to Joseph Smith, repeated this verse over a period of four years beginning September 21, 1823, and continuing until September 22, 1827, when Joseph received the ancient records.

As Joseph Smith translated the plates "through the power of God"[4] he learned that that record gave an account of a group of Israelites who were directed by the Lord to the Western Hemisphere. There they built temples patterned after Solomon's Temple in the Old Testament. They were also visited by Jesus Christ at their temple in Bountiful after his resurrection in Jerusalem (2 Nephi 5:16; 3 Nephi 11:1).

Shortly after the organization of the LDS Church in 1830, a temple was again mentioned in a revelation received by Joseph Smith: "I am Jesus Christ, the son of God; . . . I will suddenly come to my temple" (D&C 36:8).

From June 1830 to February 1831, while making revisions to the Bible, Joseph Smith received a revelation called the book of Moses. It contains a large portion of the completed temple endowment.

---

4. Every time Joseph Smith was asked how he translated the Book of Mormon, he replied, "through the power of God." This is also how he produced the book of Moses and likely the book of Abraham in the Pearl of Great Price. These books contain much of the LDS temple ceremony and were received long before the Prophet's encounter with Masonry in the early 1840s.

Newel K. Whitney Store. Joseph Smith's first residence in Kirtland, where he received revelations including certain temple procedures.

In 1832, a School of the Prophets was held in an upper room of the Newell K. Whitney Store and later in the Kirtland Temple. In a revelation, Joseph Smith was to "offer himself in prayer upon his knees before God in token or remembrance of the everlasting covenant." He was then to salute those entering with these words: "Art thou a brother or brethren? I salute you in the name of Jesus Christ." Then Joseph Smith repeated, "In token of remembrance of the everlasting covenant, in which covenant I receive you to fellowship . . . In the bonds of love, to walk in all the commandments of God blameless, in thanksgiving, for ever and ever. Amen" (D&C 88:130–33).

One of the first LDS buildings constructed was the Kirtland, Ohio, temple, a remarkable structure considering the impoverished circumstances of most members. It was started in 1833 and dedicated March 27, 1836 (D&C 109). A week later, the Savior appeared to Joseph Smith and Oliver Cowdery in the temple. Other messengers appeared: Moses, Elias, and Elijah, who restored priesthood keys, including temple and genealogy work (D&C 110). The concept of a temple and its

Kirtland Temple. The first LDS temple where early aspects of the temple ceremony were practiced and Joseph Smith and Oliver Cowdery were visited by Jesus, Moses, Elias and Elijah.

ritual was part of Mormonism years before Nauvoo and before Joseph Smith became a Mason.

The full temple ceremony developed gradually, and the Kirtland Temple is referred to in LDS history as the "Elias of temples," a forerunner to later temples. A partial endowment[5] was administered, and washings and anointings were performed. Less than two years after the dedication of this first temple, it was abandoned at the end of 1837 because of persecution and dissension within the Church. Faithful Latter-day Saints fled to Missouri. Joseph Smith escaped from death threats when his friends hid him in a coffin and he was taken away from Kirtland on a wagon on January 12, 1838. Other

5. *Endowment* is the word Joseph Smith used for the main part of the LDS ceremony, which was more fully developed in the Nauvoo period of the Church.

John C. Bennett. A Mason who converted to Mormonism and helped gain a Masonic Lodge for Nauvoo. He later turned against Joseph Smith.

temples were also planned for Missouri, with cornerstones laid in Independence in 1831 and Far West in 1838.

In the winter of 1838–39 the Latter-day Saints were driven out of Missouri and fled to Illinois and Iowa. Most Latter-day Saints stayed in Quincy, where thousands of them were welcomed with open arms and given aid, even though they outnumbered the citizens of that community. (It is interesting to note that six years later, when the Latter-day Saints were driven out of Nauvoo, the people of Quincy again helped the exiled Saints. They sent boats with supplies up the Mississippi River to Montrose, Iowa, across from Nauvoo, to aid the Saints fleeing to the West.[6])

6. When the rebuilt Nauvoo temple was dedicated in Nauvoo, the Mormon Tabernacle Choir performed at the dedication and also put on a benefit concert in Quincy in appreciation for the kindness shown by those citizens when Latter-day Saints had to evacuate Missouri and Illinois. They also became mediators when conflicts arose between Nauvoo and non-LDS communities. It is interesting to note that Quincy citizens hid and gave refuge to runaway slaves during the Civil War.

Joseph Smith rejoined his family in Quincy when he was allowed to escape after being imprisoned in Missouri jails for six months.[7] When the Latter-day Saints left Quincy during late 1839 and 1840, leaders purchased large tracts of land on credit, including the swamp-plagued, mosquito-infested village called Commerce that others did not want. After months of building canals to drain the stagnant water and make the land habitable, Joseph Smith renamed the area *Nauvoo*—a Hebrew word meaning "beautiful place"—and plans for a beautiful city with a magnificent temple to the Lord began to unfold.

On the picturesque horseshoe bend of the Mississippi[8] a few miles north of where Illinois, Missouri, and Iowa come together, Latter-day Saints began building a new gathering place. New converts flocked to Nauvoo daily, mostly from the British Isles and eastern parts of the United States. Nauvoo would grow to 12,000 inhabitants,[9] perhaps the largest city in Illinois.

A request for a Nauvoo Masonic Lodge was made with Joseph Smith's approval by John C. Bennett and other Masons. This relationship with Bennett went from a blessing to bitterness, animosity, and hate. Bennett had been a Masonic officer who had recently converted to Mormonism in 1840 and continued as a Mason. He was also instrumental in getting the State of Illinois to grant a charter allowing Mormons to establish their own city, for which the Latter-day Saints were extremely grateful. Bennett eventually became one of the leading anti-Mormons.

Joseph Smith became a Mason on March 15, 1842. The

---

7. It is believed that the reason Joseph Smith was allowed to escape, was for lack of evidence. As an escapee there was a new charge to arrest him.

8. Robert Ripley's *Believe It or Not* asks, "Which is the only town that has a straight Main Street that begins and ends at the same river?" The answer is Nauvoo, located in this horseshoe bend of the Mississippi.

9. Some accounts say Chicago was slightly larger. In any event, they were close in population. Today Nauvoo's population is 1,300, about 10 percent the size of 12,000 it was in 1846. Chicago is over five million.

Restored Nauvoo Masonic Hall. Dedicated April 5, 1844, it became the largest and most elaborate in the western United States.

number of Masons grew dramatically, with the Nauvoo Lodge eventually growing to some 1,500 members, compared to 157 in the rest of Illinois and only 2,072 in the rest of the United State.[10]

The largest and most stately Masonic Hall in the western United States, the only three-story structure in Nauvoo, was dedicated April 5, 1844, which added to the animosity and jealousy of the Masons in other Lodges. The LDS Temple was only 20 feet above the ground at that time, but became the largest building when it was dedicated in early 1846.

Four years after their arrival in Nauvoo, Joseph Smith was slain at nearby Carthage on June 27, 1844. Some Masons were suspected of having taken part.[11] Less than two years later, the Latter-day Saints started their forced exodus from

10. (Godfrey, Kenneth W., *Encyclopedia of Mormonism,* 2:527
11. A trial of those charged with killing Joseph Smith (including Masons) was held, but they were all acquitted. For the best account read Dallin H. Oaks and Marvin S. Hill, *Carthage Conspiracy.*

Nauvoo. However, this time they had completed their house of the Lord in time for the members of the Church to gain spiritual strength by partaking of the sacred temple rituals.

Receiving this holy temple ordinance was a prime factor that kept the vast majority of the members true and faithful to The Church of Jesus Christ of Latter-day Saints and enabled them to endure the trials they faced on the arduous 1,300-mile journey to the Rocky Mountains. Originally, receiving the endowment was planned before leaving Nauvoo, but atrocities against them necessitated an earlier than planned departure on February 4, 1846. Some who fled Nauvoo before receiv-

Nauvoo Temple site selected by Joseph Smith in October 1840 and cornerstone placed April 5, 1841. Restored temple dedicated by President Gordon B. Hinckley, June 27-30, 2002.

ing their endowment returned across the Mississippi during the night to receive this sustaining ordinance and then crossed back in the morning to the Iowa side of the river. There they continued their journey west, the largest mass migration in United States history.

This future location of Church headquarters was prophesied by Joseph Smith on April 5, 1842, when he said that "within five years the Saints would be in the tops of the Rocky Mountains".[12]

Without a temple on their westward journey, Brigham Young and other leaders from time to time sought a secluded spot where they could renew their covenants they had made with the Lord in the Nauvoo temple.

On July 28, four days after Brigham Young and the first company of Saints arrived in the Salt Lake Valley, he designated the site for the new temple. The abandoned Nauvoo Temple was destroyed by an arsonist in 1848, hit by a tornado in 1850, and leveled by city engineers in 1852.

By the end of 2005, there were 122 operating temples in The Church of Jesus Christ of Latter-day Saints. From June 27 to 30, 2002, LDS Church president Gordon B. Hinckley dedicated the Nauvoo Illinois Temple on the same site where the Nauvoo Temple had been left behind in 1846.

---

12. *History of the Church*, 6:225

Joseph Smith and Temple/Masonic Chronology

September 21, 1823, to September 22, 1827

Joseph Smith was made aware of the necessity of *temples* as he began his work. When Moroni appeared to him and directed him to the Book of Mormon plates, the angel also quoted Malachi, who spoke of *temple* issues:

Elijah would come and "turn the hearts of the children to their fathers." Also before the end of the world, "The Lord . . . will suddenly come to his *temple*." The Lord, after he appeared in America at the *temple* of Bountiful, considered these Malachi chapters so important that he gave them to Nephi to include in the Book of Mormon (Malachi 3–4; 3 Nephi 24–25).

June 1830 to February 1831

Making revisions to the Bible, Joseph Smith received revelations that are called the book of Moses and are found in the Pearl of Great Price. They became a major part of the *temple* endowment.

December 1830

A revelation to Joseph Smith stated, "I am Jesus Christ; . . . I will suddenly come to my *temple*" (D&C 36:8; emphasis added).

August 3, 1831

The Prophet dedicated the Independence, Missouri, *temple* site (D&C 57:4).

"February 16, 1832

Revelation on three kingdoms (D&C 76; John 5:29)"

December 27, 1832

Joseph received revelation to build a *temple* in Kirtland, Ohio (D&C 88:119).

January 3, 1833

At the School of the Prophets in Kirtland, Joseph Smith gave instruction similar to what became part of the *temple* endowment (D&C 88:130–133).

June 22, 1834

The Lord revealed, "It is expedient that . . . the first elders of my church should receive their endowment from on high, in *my house* which I have commanded to be built unto my name in the land of Kirtland" (D&C 105:33; emphasis added).

July 6, 1835

Joseph purchased ancient Egyptian papyri and translated the words of Abraham. They contained concepts that became part of the *temple* endowment.

March 27, 1836

Kirtland *Temple* dedicated by Joseph Smith (D&C 109). Miraculous angelic manifestation were reported.

April 3, 1836

Joseph and Oliver Cowdery, while kneeling in prayer in the Kirtland *Temple,* were visited by Jesus, Elias, Moses, and Elijah, who restored priesthood keys pertaining to *temple* work (D&C 110).

July 4, 1838

Joseph Smith placed cornerstones for a *temple* at Far West, Missouri.

November 1839

On his way to Washington, D.C., to petition President Martin Van Buren for redress for the wrongs received in Missouri, Joseph Smith preached in Springfield, the capitol of Illinois. There he met James Adams, a deputy grand master of the Grand *Masonic Lodge* of Illinois and a Mormon. Earlier, Adams lost an election to become governor of Illinois, but now was a probate judge. He became a lifelong friend of Joseph Smith and became branch president in Springfield and a patriarch. Judge Adams helped get the Nauvoo Charter passed and get a *Masonic Lodge* for Nauvoo. He was one of the first to receive his endowment from the Prophet in Nauvoo.

August 1, 1840

Joseph Smith announced a *temple* to be built in Nauvoo, Illinois.

August 15, 1840

Joseph Smith announced the doctrine of baptisms for the dead.

September or October, 1840

John C. Bennett, a **Mason**, visited Nauvoo and was baptized into the Church.

January 19, 1841

The Lord in a revelation said, "Let this house [*temple*] be built in my name, that I may reveal mine ordinances therein unto my people . . . things which have been kept hid from before the foundation of the world" (D&C 124:40–41).

Summer 1841

Some LDS *Masons*, including Bennett, requested a Nauvoo *Masonic Lodge*.

November 21, 1841

Brigham Young dedicated baptismal font in basement of the Nauvoo *Temple*.

March 15, 1842

Masonic Lodge was formed in Nauvoo. Joseph Smith and Sidney Rigdon became Third Degree *Masons.* Nauvoo soon had 1,500 *Masons.*

May 4, 1842

The first endowments were given by Joseph Smith in his office at the Red Brick Store in Nauvoo. They were given to Judge James Adams of Springfield, Patriarch Hyrum Smith, Bishops Newell K. Whitney and George Miller, and President (of the Twelve) Brigham Young, Elders Heber C. Kimball (also of the Twelve), William Law, and William Marks.

June 26, 1842

Having been disfellowshipped earlier, John C. Bennett was excommunicated from the Church. He was also expelled from the *Masonic Lodge.*

Nauvoo Red Brick Store. This is where Joseph Smith administered the temple endowment in Nauvoo to Church leaders because the temple was not ready.

August 1842

The *Masonic Lodge* at Quincy protested granting a lodge in Nauvoo. The Nauvoo Lodge was suspended, but an investigation showed there were no irregularities, and the lodge was reinstated.

October 1843

With *Masons* complaining throughout Illinois, the Grand Lodge held another investigation of the Nauvoo Lodge. They found no problems but suspected something must be wrong, and there was another temporary suspension.

Early 1844

The Nauvoo *Masonic Lodge* was severed from the Illinois Grand Lodge. Without official approval the Nauvoo *Masons* carried on.

April 5, 1844

A beautiful Nauvoo *Masonic Hall* was dedicated. Only one

non-Mormon from another Illinois Lodge attended. He was expelled from that Lodge.

June 27, 1844

Joseph Smith and his brother Hyrum were killed at Carthage Jail. Some feel the Prophet began to give the *Masonic* distress call as he faced the mob.

April 10, 1845

Brigham Young requested that the *Masonic Lodge* be suspended. The building became a social hall. It is restored today, and missionaries hold nightly musicals there.

December 1845 through August 1846

As portions of the Nauvoo *Temple* were completed, the rooms were used for endowments. There was a rush by the Saints to get *temple* ordinances, because Brigham Young agreed that Mormons would leave Nauvoo for the West in the late spring of 1846. The endowment was needed to get them through the trying times ahead and give them strength to build a Zion of their own away from mobs.

February 4, 1846

As atrocities against the Latter-day Saints increased, Brigham Young decided that to avoid more bloodshed, they must start leaving earlier. The next six months, hundreds of wagons waited in line to get a barge to cross the Mississippi River. *Temple* endowments continued night and day throughout the summer.

April 30 through May 3, 1846

In succeeding sessions the almost completed Nauvoo *Temple* was dedicated by Orson Hyde, Joseph Young and Wilford Woodruff.

Remains of the Nauvoo Temple. After the Latter-day Saints left Nauvoo, it was set on fire by arsonists in 1848 and destroyed by a tornado in 1850.

September 10 through 17, 1846

In the "Battle of Nauvoo," with a militia of over a thousand shelling the city and killing two, the few remaining Saints were driven out and the Nauvoo *Temple* fell silent. It was immediately desecrated by the mob.

July 28, 1847

Four days after the Saints arrived in the Salt Lake Valley, Brigham Young selected the spot for a *temple*.

October 9, 1848

Arsonists set fire to the Nauvoo *Temple*, destroying the interior, leaving only standing walls.

May 27, 1850

A tornado knocked over three walls, and the remaining

wall was declared a hazard and torn down. The stones are in various buildings in Nauvoo today.

June 27 through 30, 2002

The Nauvoo Illinois *Temple* was dedicated by President Gordon B. Hinckley after it was rebuilt to the grandeur of the original. (Some of the foregoing information came from Kenneth W. Godfrey, *Encyclopedia of Mormonism*, 2: 527-528)

The Salt Lake Temple was dedicated April 6 through 24, 1893. Occasionally LDS Masons have been ordinance workers in LDS temples.

Frequent Charges and Answers

1. Is the claim of critics valid that Joseph Smith stole the LDS temple ceremony from the Masons?

For starters, why would Joseph Smith have to steal ideas? He had already produced hundreds of pages of new holy writ. The late LDS apostle Bruce R. McConkie pointed out that Joseph Smith "has given to our present world more holy scripture than any single prophet who ever lived; . . . more than the total of the dozen most prolific prophet penmen of the past".[13]

Today, previous critical theories that tried to explain Joseph Smith's accomplishments are being discredited by reputable LDS and non-LDS scholars. Most non-Mormon academic historians who have made the study of Mormonism one of their fields of expertise attribute Joseph Smith's phenomenal achievements to his brilliant mind. This, these professors claim, is how Joseph Smith produced the Book of Mormon, the Doctrine and Covenants, Pearl of Great Price, and his changes to the Bible called the Joseph Smith Translation (JST). They praise Joseph Smith but avoid the issue of divine revelations. The speeches given by most of the non-Mormon presenters at the 2005 Library of Congress reflected this view.[14]

An example of this humanistic view of Joseph Smith's

---

13. *Ensign,* May 1976, 95.
14. For further reading of all the speeches see Welch, John W., "The Worlds of Joseph Smith," *BYU Studies, Vol. 4, 2005.*

achievements was made by Harold Bloom, considered by many to be America's foremost literary critic and best known man of letters. Bloom appeared in *Trail of Hope* and *American Prophet*, PBS Television specials, and praised Joseph Smith and Mormonism in those films and in his book *The American Religion*.[15]

Dr. Bloom said of Joseph Smith, "There is no other figure remotely like him in our entire national history, and it is unlikely that anyone like him can ever come again. He transcends Emerson and Whitman." However, Bloom did not credit the Prophet's work to revelation from God instead calling it "the religion making genius of Joseph Smith."[16]

This secular explanation prevailed at the 2005, three-day Symposium on Joseph Smith at the Library of Congress in Washington, D.C., in recognition of the 200th anniversary of his birth. The library officials, with the approval of a congressional committee and the cooperation of Brigham Young University, scheduled this event by stating that a person who made such a great impact on the nation and world deserved to be examined.

Half of those who presented papers were non-Mormons. They praised Joseph Smith's remarkable achievements, but not one of them gave credit to God as the source.[17]

If this latest reasoning has merit—that the origin of Joseph Smith's prodigious accomplishments were products of his mind only—would it not have been much easier and safer for

---

15. Prior to giving a lecture on Joseph Smith at the University of Utah, Bloom told a reporter, "I have the most passionate appreciation for [Joseph Smith]. . . . I'm not sure if I had been born some denomination Christian, rather than Jew, I would not have wound up a Mormon" (*Salt Lake Tribune,* November 11, 1990, 2E). Of Bloom's some twenty-four books, perhaps his most famous one is the *The Book of J,* which is an alternate translation of parts of the Old Testament that speaks at length of Enoch. Joseph Smith also restored three chapters dealing with Enoch, which have parallels with the *Book of J.* The Old Testament has only a few verses about Enoch.

16. Bloom, 126

17. Ibid.

Joseph Smith to produce a completely original LDS temple ceremony? Then he would not need to correct any indirect procedural similarities to Masonry. Joseph Smith could have avoided much criticism. However, since he knew when he received revelation from the Lord, criticism did not concern him.

Joseph Smith often came across biblical passages or other material that interested him or that he did not understand. By asking the Lord, he received clarification. Many of the revelations in the Doctrine and Covenants and other teachings came to the Prophet in this manner. This pattern of asking the Lord for the meaning of things led to the doctrines he taught his followers.

When Joseph Smith was exposed to Masonic ritual, he certainly followed this procedure and asked the Lord, "What is this all about? Is there any truth in this?" as he had done with other issues throughout his life. He would have done this especially when he learned that Masons claimed their signs and symbols came from the biblical temple of Solomon. Then revelation from God helped him sort things out and finalize the LDS temple endowment. In the process he discovered that the teaching method of Masonic ritual had great merit, but not the Masonic meanings.

Joseph's close friend, and also a Mason in Nauvoo, Franklin D. Richards, who became an apostle in 1849, stated: "Joseph, the Prophet, was aware that there were some things about Masonry that had come down from the beginning and he desired to know what they were, hence the lodge. Masons knew some keys of knowledge appertaining to Masonry were lost. Joseph enquired of the Lord . . . and he revealed to him the [temple ceremony]."[18] Thus, most Masons in Nauvoo looked to Joseph Smith to supply what was missing from their ritual.

Yes, the mind of Joseph Smith, as with all humans, was involved in all he did. However, the LDS temple ceremony came

18. Cited in Bradley, Don,"The Grand Fundamental Principles of Mormonism," *Dialogue* (April 2006} 4.

through Joseph Smith's mind *and* through inspiration from God, as did the scriptures and teachings he gave to the Church as we shall see from the following questions.

2. Since prophets and apostles ended with the Bible, how can Latter-day Saints claim their temple ceremony came from God?

Those who maintain this position ignore what the Bible has to say: "Surely the Lord God will do nothing, but he revealeth his secrets unto his servants, the prophets" (Amos 3:7). Those who claim prophets and apostles do not exist in our day ignore this verse; and they don't believe Paul, who stated that the Savior's Church must "be built upon the foundation of apostles and prophets, Jesus Christ himself being the chief cornerstone" (Ephraim 2:20).

Furthermore, Paul proclaimed that apostles and prophets must continue until "we all come to a unity of faith" (Ephraim 4:11-13). Since the world is far from "a unity of faith," apostles and prophets are definitely needed. Where in scripture does it say that prophets and apostles must end with the Bible? I have found no such statements.[19] Fundamental to The Church of

---

19. Critics of the idea of a continuation of prophets after the Bible like to quote the last two verses of the New Testament in which John said, "If any shall add unto these things, God shall add unto him the plagues that are written in this book" (Revelation 22:18). Some say this means there should be no scripture or prophets. However, a similar verse in the Old Testament, Deuteronomy 4:2, says essentially the same thing. Thus it is just as reasonable to claim that any books beyond the book of Deuteronomy are invalid. John had no idea that hundreds of years after he wrote his manuscript it would be placed at the end of a volume of books called the New Testament. The word *Bible* means collection of books, not one book. Some Christians did not accept the Epistles of John or his book of Revelation. However, some New Testament books were written later than Revelation. Dozens of books mentioned in the Bible are considered scripture that are nowhere to be found today. For a list of such missing biblical books, see Scharffs, Gilbert W., *The Missionary's Little Book of Answers* (2002), 63-65.

Jesus Christ of Latter-day Saints is that we are led by apostles and prophets, beginning with Joseph Smith. "We believe in the same organization that existed in the Primitive Church, namely, apostles, prophets, pastors, teachers, evangelists, and so forth" (6th Article of Faith).

The need for inspiration from God is needed today in our nuclear age, even more than in times past. No mortal mind could produce what Joseph Smith did, including sacred LDS temple ceremonies.

3. Why did Masons in Illinois turn against Joseph Smith if he did not plagiarize their ritual?

So-called "similarities" between Masonic and LDS ceremonies were not an issue during the Nauvoo period. The animosity that developed between Mormons and non-Nauvoo Masons in Illinois were the same reasons the population at large became mostly anti-LDS. Mormons previously had to abandon New York, Ohio and Missouri where there was no Masonic issue.

Tremendous growth, both in population and economic strengths causing jealousy in nearby communities was a significant reason. Also, misrepresentation of the beginnings of the practice of plural marriage, the LDS Church claiming to be God's official organization and having living prophets, and distortions and lies about the Saints written by Thomas Sharp, publisher of the *Warsaw Signal,* were factors. A primary cause that brought the animosities to a head was the outrage caused by the destruction of a libelous, anti-Mormon press in Nauvoo, although destruction of libelous presses was not uncommon on the western frontier of the United States.[20]

Non-Nauvoo Masons in other lodges in Illinois had their own reasons for anger with the Mormons. They worried about the large number of Mormon Masons and were also concerned

20. For a complete account read Leonard, Glen M., *Nauvoo: A Place of Peace, a People of Promise,* Deseret Book and BYU Press [2002], 508-50.

about the legitimacy of the Lodge at Nauvoo. New Lodges traditionally needed to be sponsored by an existing Lodge if they received permission from a state's Grand Master, who was Abraham Jonas for the state of Illinois. The Bodley Lodge No. 1 in Quincy did not want to sponsor a Lodge in Nauvoo, but Jonas went ahead anyway. Some feel that he acted on his own to gain Mormon support for his political ambitions.

Other Masons were concerned that Joseph Smith and his counselor Sidney Rigdon were made Third-Degree Masons in two days, the highest level in the York Rite. Such quick advancement was highly unusual. (Today, some critics erroneously claim Joseph Smith became a Thirty-Second degree Mason, which is possible in the Scottish Rite, but this type of Masonry was not yet in the United States.)

Support for the Nauvoo Lodge was withdrawn while an investigation was launched into its procedures. The investigators found everything in order, and the Nauvoo Lodge was officially approved after a year's waiting time to be sure no problems developed. Jonas wrote of the Nauvoo Lodge, "Never in my life did I witness a better dressed or more orderly and well-behaved assemblage." Two other Lodges, with mostly LDS Masons, were soon functioning across the river in Montrose and Keokuk. A newly erected, impressive Lodge Hall (the largest in western America) was dedicated in Nauvoo in April 1844. By then the Lodge was no longer recognized by other lodges.[21]

4. Since Joseph Smith claimed to restore the Church that Christ established, why did he get involved with another religion?

Masonry in no way claims to be a religion. Members of other Christian groups are Masons, as are followers of other

21. Godfrey, Kenneth W., *Encyclopedia of Mormonism*, 2:529

non-Christian religions. A Mason must believe in a Supreme being; atheists are not allowed. Masonry is a fraternal organization. Many prominent Americans were Masons, including George Washington and Franklin D. Roosevelt and eleven other presidents of the United States; Benjamin Franklin and other founding fathers, including eight signers of the Declaration of Independence; and Winston Churchill.

The Worshipful Master Steven H. Mesnick describes "Freemasonry as a charitable organization . . . . It is the largest contributor of blood to the Red Cross and other blood banks. The Shriners [a division of Freemasonry], have Burn Institutes and Hospitals for Crippled Children (at which all services are free).

"It is a social organization to cultivate friendships. . . . One of our basic principles is that [members] seek a greater knowledge of the universe and their place in it. . . . Our ritual (which is rich, complex and endlessly inspiring) stresses certain truths upon which, on reflection, men of many different backgrounds, religions, and opinions can agree—and have agreed for centuries. This ritual forms the focus of our regular meetings."

No wonder Joseph Smith found Masonry attractive. His 13th Article of Faith states: "We believe in being honest, true, chaste, benevolent, virtuous, and in doing good to all men. . . . If there is anything virtuous, lovely, or of good report or praiseworthy, we seek after these things."[22] This fundamental declaration of an LDS teaching sounds a lot like what Masons believe.

Joseph Smith had connections to Masonry long before

22. Of Joseph Smith's 13 Articles of Faith, literary critic Harold Bloom wrote: "The Wentworth Letter [including the 13 Articles of Faith] prints in six pages and is marked by the dignity of a simple eloquence, and by self-possession of a religious innovator who is so secure in the truth of his doctrine that he can state its pith with almost miraculous economy. . . . Smith was an authentic religious genius, unique in our national history" (Bloom, 82).

Nauvoo. His father and brother Hyrum joined Masonry when they lived in New York, as had many New Englanders. Other LDS leaders such as Heber C. Kimball, Newell K. Whitney, the Prophet's uncle John Smith, and Lucius Scovil were Masons. Scovil donated the land for the Masonic Hall on Main Street in Nauvoo and was a leader in the Lodge. (Tourists in Nauvoo today can visit the restored Masonic Hall, where LDS missionaries put on a nightly musical production, *Rendezvous in Old Nauvoo*, and can get free cookies at the Scovil bakery next door.)

Such friends and family made Joseph Smith feel comfortable around Masons. James Adams, a Mason and probate judge in Springville, the capital of Illinois, converted to Mormonism and was influential in convincing Joseph Smith that a Masonic Lodge in Nauvoo should be pursued.

Some additional reasons why Joseph Smith became a Mason were compiled by LDS historians Donald Q. Cannon, Kenneth W. Godfrey and Mervin B. Hogan (who is a Mason):

a) Perhaps because of his recent suffering and imprisonment in Missouri, Joseph Smith wanted to secure friendship, acceptance and protection.

b) Since many leading politicians in Illinois were Masons, the Prophet wanted to gain their support and cooperation.

c) There was an attraction and admiration for Masonry's cultural and moral values and its example of service and brotherhood.

d) Joseph wanted and needed social interaction, since he was a warm, friendly, outgoing person.

e) Enemies persecuted both Mormons and Masons, and these two groups needed each other. A scandal in Masonry in the 1830s had made Masons unpopular in the United States.

Temple of Solomon. Both Masons and Mormons have an interest in this temple but with completely different interpretations of the significance of that Jewish structure. Hiram Abiff, significant to Masons, was the chief builder of the temple, and one of the legends of the Masonic distress call involves him.

f) Joseph Smith desired to learn all he could about Masonry, recognizing value in the methodology of its ancient practices. Since Joseph was restoring biblical religion, he was interested in Masonic teachings since certain aspects go back to stone masons who worked on Solomon's Temple.

However, research since then indicates that Masonic and especially Latter-day Saint ritual have beginnings long before Solomon's Temple, as will be shown in question 15 of this study.

5. How did those who were Masons before becoming Latter-day Saints react to LDS rituals in Joseph Smith's day?

There are accounts of Masons who were pleased that the LDS endowment did not negate Masonic beliefs and went beyond what Masonry taught. The Latter-day Saint Masons that I know today feel the same, and a few are ordinance workers in LDS temples. As previously shown, Masonry contains strict rules for living an honorable life. So does the LDS temple ceremony, which also emphasizes God's purposes and rewards beyond this life.

Apostle Heber C. Kimball, who had been a Mason long before Nauvoo and who later became a counselor to Brigham Young, once stated that because of its high moral teachings, a man should be a Mason for six months before becoming a Mormon.

It seems that some of the 1,500 Mormon Masons in and around Nauvoo would have been outraged if Joseph Smith had made improper use of Masonic rituals. It's possible that my research on this matter may have missed examples of disaffection with Mormonism over the "similarity" issue. Instead, I found some became alienated from the Church for other reasons. People often leave a church organization for a number of factors, such as being offended, or behavioral issues, as was the case with John C. Bennett.

Bennett had been a Masonic leader before he came to Nauvoo and was instrumental in getting the Masonic Lodge in Nauvoo. Bennett had been quartermaster for the State of Illinois. He was a convert to the LDS Church in 1840 and was able get the Nauvoo City Charter passed by the Illinois Legislature. This gave Mormons the right to their own military, courts and a university. He also became the first Mayor of Nauvoo.[23]Bennett committed adultery and took advantage of his positions of power, seducing women, and falsely claiming such actions were approved by Joseph Smith. It was also found that he had abandoned his wife (to whom he was still legally married) and his children in the East. Further investigation into his past revealed accusations of misconduct in various places he had lived, including expulsion from an Ohio Masonic Lodge.

John C. Bennett was excommunicated from the Church and expelled from the Masonic Lodge in Nauvoo. He at first seemed remorseful, admitting the charges against him. Ben-

23. Bennett also for a brief time became an assistant to Joseph Smith, taking the place of the ailing Sidney Rigdon, the Prophet's first counselor.

nett also wrote a certificate that Joseph Smith had *not* taught the things that he previously claimed.

A short time later, Bennett became a bitter enemy of Joseph Smith and the LDS Church. He lied to the Missouri governor, Lilburn W. Boggs, claiming Joseph Smith had been responsible for the assassination attempt that had wounded Boggs in 1842. It was Boggs who had issued the extermination order that drove the Latter-day Saints from Missouri. Although the persecuted and exiled Mormons would have been logical suspects, I have not seen any evidence that Joseph Smith was responsible.[24] In fact, Joseph Smith was acquitted of this charge in a district court in Springfield, Illinois, in 1843. The courtroom was in the same building that housed the offices of Abraham Lincoln. Lincoln's wife, Mary Todd, attended the trial. While in Springfield, Joseph Smith was invited to speak at a Sunday service in the state capitol building.

Bennett wrote a bitter anti-Mormon book, *Story of the Saints,* that was quoted in newspapers in the United States and abroad. He did not make an issue of "similarities" between Masonic rites and the LDS Temple ceremony. He certainly would have emphasized this if he had thought this was a valid point.

6. What is the relationship between Mormons and Masons since Nauvoo?

As hostilities accelerated between Latter-day Saints and non-LDS people, the Mormons agreed to leave Nauvoo in the spring of 1846, "when water flows and grass grows," so that their animals could graze the prairie and the Saints could rely on streams for water. The looting and burning of outlying LDS communities abated for a short time but resumed early in 1846.

24. In 1976, the Missouri legislature rescinded the 1838 extermination order and apologized for associated past actions. In 2004, the state of Illinois in its first draft of a resolution apologized but in the final version issued regrets for the 1846 Mormon expulsion from Illinois (Leonard, 351).

**Salt Lake Masonic Lodge. Dedicated
November 27, 1927. Some Latter-day Saints
are members of this or other lodges.**

To avoid bloodshed, Brigham Young led the first company of Latter-day Saints from Nauvoo on February 4, in the dead of winter. Almost a year earlier, on April 11, he had asked that the Lodge in Nauvoo be discontinued. A year before that, the Grand Lodge in Illinois had ended its recognition of the Nauvoo Lodge a few months before Joseph Smith's assassination in 1844. There is evidence that some in the mob at Carthage that killed the Prophet were Masons.

The four presidents of the LDS Church who succeeded Joseph Smith were Masons, but they discontinued their association with Masonry after the Prophet's death. After the Saints arrived in the Salt Lake Valley in 1847, there was no Masonic Lodge for a decade, and when one was established, it did not involve the Saints.

In 1857, United States President James Buchanan sent 2,500 troops, about one-half of the U. S. Army, led by general Albert Sidney Johnston, to put down a "rebellion" by the Mormons in the recently formed Utah Territory.[25] Before the troops entered the Salt Lake Valley, a treaty was arranged so that the army would not stop in Salt Lake City, but continue on. They settled about forty-five miles to the southwest where they set up their encampment.

Here, some of the soldiers who were Masons erected a crude adobe building in 1859, ironically called the Rocky Mountain Lodge No. 205, Missouri register, which included former enemies from that state. A year later the Civil War began and the Lodge ceased to exist when the troops were called back to the States.

In 1869, when the first transcontinental railroad crossed Utah, Salt Lake City began to have an increasing non-LDS population. Soon the first Masonic Hall in Salt Lake City was established.[26] Over the years, several other locations became home for Masons in the city, each building increasing in size and grandeur. The current huge and elegant structure, which houses several Lodges, was dedicated November 20, 1927, at 650 East South Temple Street and is comparable in size to the Salt Lake LDS Temple, located a mile to the west.

---

25. Since Utah was a United States Territory, officials were appointed by the federal government. This included Brigham Young as governor. From the beginning there was conflict between Latter-day Saints and the federally appointed judges. One judge, William W. Drummond, who was appointed, had deserted his wife in Chicago and brought a mistress that he had sit next to him on the bench as he passed out sentences against Mormons. Drummond, sensing LDS resentment, abandoned his post and retuned to Washington, giving his excuse to United States President James Buchanan, that Mormons in Utah were in a state of rebellion. Buchanan, without any investigation, sent 2,500 United States troops. When it was found that there was no rebellion, the Eastern press attacked the president, calling his actions "Buchanan's Blunder."

26. The first Masonic Lodge was at 128 South Main, just south of where the then-LDS owned Zions Bank still stands today. Here the Mt. Moriah and Wasatch Lodges were organized.

In 2005, a few of my colleagues and I had an extensive tour of the building. One of our participants was both a Mormon and a Mason, and we were all treated with respect. We were taken into some of the rooms where Masonic rites are performed, but I could not spot anything in the building that had any resemblance to LDS temples.

I have found no statements by LDS Church officials banning Latter-day Saints from being Masons.[27] Over the years in Utah there was some friction between the two groups due to misunderstanding and perceived problems. For a time Masons were not allowed to become Latter-day Saints and remain Masons. This did not apply to areas outside Utah.

In 1984, Masonic leaders, after a thorough study of the charges that had circulated, came to the conclusion that their concerns were not valid and Masons could be Mormons. In 2007, a Latter-day Saint who is Worshipful Senior Grand Warden is scheduled to become the first LDS Grand Master in Utah. There are some 2,000 Masons in Utah today, a much lower rate than most areas in the United States.

In 2005, I taught the course "Teachings of the Prophet Joseph Smith" at the BYU Semester in Nauvoo. I was surprised to meet one of my students that I had taught several years earlier at the LDS Institute of Religion adjacent to the University of Utah in Salt Lake City. He had become a Mason and was now residing in Nauvoo, where he could study firsthand records of Masonry in the Nauvoo period of the Church. When I asked

---

27. In general conference on April 9, 1911, a reference to Masonry was made in a statement by the First Presidency in response to false statements made in national magazines about the LDS Church. "Because of their Masonic characters, the ceremonies in the temple are sacred and not for the public. But there is nothing disloyal in them, as so often asserted, nor in their performance is there the slightest departure from the principles of decorum and propriety."(This was part of a lengthy statement about many issues not related to Masonry and was printed as a pamphlet. It also appeared in the *Improvement Era*, June 1911, 719-24.)

him why, he responded that he wanted to lay to rest all of the accusations of "similarity" he had been exposed to before. He assured me he found no conflict. Today, the nearest Lodge to Nauvoo is in Carthage, about twenty-three miles away.

7. What are some differences between Mormon and Masonic rituals?

Critics are quick to bring up similarities, mostly erroneously perceived, but neglect the vast differences.

a) Covenants in the LDS temples are between man and God; in Masonry they are between man and man.

b) In an LDS temple everyone is equal before God; rank in Masonry is very important.

c) Jesus Christ is the central focus in an LDS temple. (Critics claim Joseph Smith received his anti-Trinitarian idea of the Godhead from Masons. However, Masonic ritual refers only to an impersonal God.)

d) Adam and Eve, representing men and women of the world, are important in the LDS ceremony; a male figure, Hiram Abiff, is the hero in Masonic rites. He was the chief builder of Solomon's Temple (1 Kings 7:13, 40, 45; Also called Hurum, 2 Chronicles 2;13; 4:11, 16).

e) The LDS temple includes marriages that continue after death and the sealing of families in an eternal relationship; there is no mention of this in Masonry.

f) The LDS temple includes a plan that enables all mankind to return to God by performing ordinances for those who are deceased; Masonry does not deal with an afterlife or proxy rituals for the dead.

g) Priesthood, or authority from God, is stressed; in Masonry there is only minor reference to authority and no mention of Aaron or Melchizedek.

h) Women have an equal part in LDS rituals; women do not take part in Masonic rites. There are women and youth clubs.

i) Mormonism is a church; Masons are a fraternal organization.

j) Latter-day Saint temples have a baptismal font resting on the backs of twelve carved oxen representing the twelve tribes of Israel; even though there was a font on the "backs of twelve oxen" in Solomon's Temple, built by Hiram Abiff, there is no such font in Masonic buildings.

k) Anointing with oil is an old Jewish, Christian and Islamic tradition, but not found in Masonry.

Although Masons do not have a baptismal font upon the backs of twelve symbolic oxen, Latter-day Saint and Masonic ritual have a common point of reference in Solomon's Temple that came to light in Nauvoo. However, the Mormon rites took a completely different direction based on the fact that LDS temple rituals began to emerge from the Church's beginnings. Furthermore, Mormon ritual is based on many other happenings in the Old and New Testaments of the Bible and on events in the Western Hemisphere (as recorded in the Book of Mormon) which the Savior visited after his resurrection.

The accuracy of Joseph Smith's development of the LDS temple ceremony is supported by nonbiblical sources that predate Solomon's Temple. Joseph Smith could only have known of these earlier concepts through revelation from God.

The Church of Jesus Christ of Latter-day Saints claims to be the restoration of a plan that was first developed in our premortal existence. On earth it was first implemented by God the Father and Jesus Christ through Adam and Eve. It continued throughout the Old Testament under the leadership of such prophets as Noah, Abraham, Isaac, Jacob, and Malachi. This accounts for elements of the temple ceremony being found here and there in ancient practices, even in pre-Solomon times.

In the meridian of time, Jesus Christ was born, and again organized his Church. Through his death and suffering on the cross, the Son of God brought about resurrection and immortality for all mankind and eternal life for those who keep his commandments and sacred covenants (John 14:15).

After centuries of man-made changes, deletions and additions, Christ's authorized Church ceased to exist until the full and complete ordinances were restored through Joseph Smith. Under the direction of today's prophet, these solemn practices are continued in temples of The Church of Jesus Christ of Latter-day Saints.

8. Because secrecy is contrary to Christianity, does that not invalidate the LDS temple ceremony?

When Masonry in its current form began is not agreed upon. It began sometime around A.D. 1640 in Scotland and England. In 1717, four Lodges joined together in London to form a "Grand Lodge."

Neither Mormons nor Masons are a secret organization. A Masonic leader, Steven H. Mesnick, put it clearly: "Freemasonry is NOT a secret organization. A secret organization is one that keeps its existence, or a least its membership, a secret. Everyone knows Freemasonry exists. Freemasonry is an *organization with secrets.*"

The same could be said about the LDS Church, except Mormons prefer using "sacred" instead of "secret." The covenants Latter-day Saints make in temples are all principles taught in the Bible, such as keeping God's commandments, living chaste lives and building up God's kingdom on earth in preparation for Christ's Second Coming. With these covenants, certain signs and symbols are used, which are not to be spoken of outside the temple.

However, those who say secrecy was not part of former-day Christianity do not understand the Bible. One wonders about when the disciples asked Christ, "Why speakest thou unto them in parables?" He answered and said unto them, "Because it is given unto you to know the *mysteries* of the kingdom of heaven, but to them it is not given (Matt 13:11; emphasis added). Christ also said, "I have yet many things to say unto you, but ye cannot bear them now" (John 16:12; the same idea is repeated in Mark 4:11 and Luke 8:10).

Paul, writing to the Romans, said, "I would not . . . that ye should be ignorant of this *mystery* (Romans 11:25; emphasis added). In the same letter Paul spoke of the "preaching of Christ, according to the revelation of the *mystery*, which was kept *secret* since the world began" (Rom. 16:25; emphasis added).

What did John mean when he said, "He that hath an ear, let him hear what the Spirit saith unto the churches; to him that overcometh will I give to eat of the *hidden* manna"? (Revelation 2:17; emphasis added). And Paul said, "We speak the wisdom of God in a *mystery*, even the *hidden* wisdom, which God ordained before the world unto our glory" (1 Corinthians 2:7; emphasis added).

Paul also said, "[Let us be] stewards of the *mysteries* of God" (1 Corinthians 4:1; emphasis added) and "by revelation [God] made known unto me the *mystery* (Ephraim 3:3 ; emphasis added). As Amos was previously quoted in a different context, "Surely the Lord God will do nothing, but he revealeth his *secret* unto his servants the Prophets" (Amos 3:7 ; emphasis added). There are many such scriptures. It is easy to make a case that some in the early Christian church taught things others did not receive.

Critics have tried to prove that Christ was against secrecy, quoting the Savior when he said, "In secret I have said nothing" (John 18:20). In the same context he also said, "Why askest thou me? Ask them which heard me," as if to say, "I don't need to testify against myself; the burden of proof is on you." Christ added, "If I have spoken evil, bear witness of the evil" (John 18:21-23).

9. Why are signs and symbols necessary in making covenants?

They are part of life. The words we use (oral and written) in communicating with one another are signs and symbols. This method of dealing with others is in our justice system, graduations, coronations, swearing-in ceremonies, and code words to access private information on computers.

Most religions use signs and symbols such as baptism, communion, last rites, bar and bas mitzva, etc.[28] However, symbols without a message or meaning are useless. Words in a foreign language mean nothing to those who do not know that language. The signs and symbols in the LDS temple ceremonies, combined with covenanting with God to live righteously, have eternal significance.

10. What is the difference between covenants and signs and symbols?

There are two aspects of Masonic and Latter-day Saint ritual: The *message* (the meaning) and the *messenger* or methodology (signs and symbols). Which is more important? Obviously, the *message*. Symbols without a message or meaning are useless.

As far as the Latter-day Saint temple endowment (the *mes-*

---

28. This is a rite of passage for boys and girls in Judaism when they reach age thirteen.

sage) is concerned, it was mostly in place prior to the Nauvoo period of the Church. The *message* is the heart of the temple ceremony. Although of ancient origin, it is unique to the LDS Church in our day, but most of the temple ceremony can be found in the Bible, the Book of Mormon, the Pearl of Great Price and numerous ancient texts that preceded Solomon's time. (See questions 13, 14 and 17 for further information.)

Most other ancient texts were not known or available in Joseph Smith's day. This is strong evidence that inspiration from God was involved in the LDS temple endowment *message*. The *message* is completely different from Masonry, according to those who are both Masons and Mormons that I have talked to or read about.

11. Aren't symbols on early Latter-day Saint temples copied from Masonry?

Similar symbols are used by Mormons and Masons, but they are also found throughout the world. There probably is not a symbol anywhere that has a single meaning. Words, as well as other symbols, have different definitions. For example, the word *gift* in English means "a present," but in the German language it means "poison." This created a problem after World War II, when relief packages arrived in Germany marked "Gift from the USA."

An example of a similar symbol having two meanings is the swastika. It is identified with Nazi Germany and is also prevalent on Navajo Indian blankets in the southwest area of the USA and elsewhere. Are Navajos Nazis?

The "All-Seeing Eye," representing God's omniscience and omnipotence, is found on LDS and Masonic buildings but is also used by older civilizations, especially Egyptians. If you use a magnifying glass, the "All-Seeing Eye" is very clear on the back of the United States dollar bill just above the unfinished

Symbols from the Latter-day Saint Nauvoo Temple.

pyramid.

The same may be said of the honeybee and the beehive. They are widespread icons of work and industry. The honeybee is mentioned in the Book of Mormon (Ether 2:3) and is the source for Utah being called the Beehive State.

Clasped hands representing brotherly love are found on tombstones of deceased people who are neither LDS or Masons. The fact that this symbol is on female graves is evidence that the clasped hand symbol is not Masonic in origin, since Masonry only applies to men. Five-pointed stars that point downward have become symbols of Satan worship in our day. Historian Matthew B. Brown has pointed out that the first book associating such stars with the devil was published in France by a defrocked priest in 1854. By this time the Nauvoo Temple had come and gone. Mormonism and Masonry are the antitheses of Satan worship. Both groups are adamantly opposed to anything having to do with the occult.

These inverted stars, also called pentagrams, were used by early Christians as a sacred representation of Jesus Christ, the downward point symbolic of the Messiah pouring light upon the inhabitants of the earth. The Savior called himself "the bright and morning star" (Revelation 22:16). This symbolism became lost in traditional Christianity but was restored in Mormonism.

In 1840, Parley P. Pratt, of the Quorum of the Twelve, wrote in a Church periodical in England:

> Now the bright and morning Star
> Spreads its glorious light afar.
> Kindles up the rising dawn
> Of that bright millennial morn.

Historian Brown has also pointed out that military uniforms and the flag of the United States have used the inverted star in the past. Today, the United States Medal of Honor has an inverted star on it. Inverted stars are also found in some of the older cathedrals in Europe.

Likewise, sunstones and moonstones do not have evil meanings. The Bible speaks of the sun, moon and stars representing heavenly bodies (1 Corinthians 15:40–42). Some of the stars on the Salt Lake Temple point up.

Because the cross was used in ancient pagan worship, Brown stated, it certainly does not make those Christians who revere the cross today Satan worshippers. Likewise Latter-day Saints should not be called Satan worshippers because they have pentagrams on their temples.

12. What have Masons who are also LDS said about the two ceremonies?

Latter-day Saint Mason Greg Kearny, who is heavily involved in both groups, says, "While both rituals teach great truths, the truths they teach are different. . . . Joseph Smith served as chaplain of the Nauvoo Rising Sun Lodge . . . and as such had occasion to see the remarkable way that the Masonic ritual is used to teach complex ideas by means of ritualistic repetition of information." Kearny goes on to explain that there were many foreigners who did not know English well and many Americans who had little formal education Symbolism made temple concepts easier to understand.

Kearny also feels that since Nauvoo had Masons who were accustomed to the Masonic teaching style, this allowed those men to look beyond the teaching methodology (the *messenger*) and focus on the LDS endowment (*message*) and not get sidetracked (fairlds.org/apol).

D. Charles Pyle, a practicing Mormon and a Mason, has said, "The rituals of the temple and the rituals of Masonry are not the same." He added, "Joseph Smith did serve as Installing Chaplain for the Rising Sun Lodge [in Nauvoo], but was not an officer of said Lodge. He was appointed by the Grand Master [Jonas] for the purpose of installation of officers of that Lodge. To say that he had many opportunities to observe the ritual, as a Chaplain, during Degree conferrals, and to offer that as grounds for using the ceremonies of Masonry to fabricate his temple ceremonies, or even implying such, is not correct and is rather irresponsible in my view" (fairlds.org/apol).

It has been said in several LDS publications that Joseph Smith attended only three Masonic meetings. Recent research of Nauvoo records seems to indicate that the number might have been as high as twenty-five.

Mormon scholar Mervin B. Hogan, a University of Utah professor who worked in the Salt Lake Temple and was also a Mason for over fifty years, stated emphatically, "No Mason—or anyone else—acquainted with the rituals of the Order can honestly claim there is the slightest resemblance of the ordinances or procedures [of the LDS endowment ceremony] to anything presented in a Symbolic Lodge of Freemasonry".[29]

George Harris, a Mason who left the LDS Church said,

29. "The Historicity of the Alleged Masonic Influence on Mormonism, pp 17, 30-31 [Jan 15, 1984]; cited in Gilbert W. Scharffs, *The Truth About the Godmakers,*179

"The signs and tokens taught in the temple were unique to Mormonism."

13. How can Latter-day Saints claim the temple endowment is inspired when there have been changes over the years?

The endowment (the *message*) has NOT been changed, but the teaching methodology (the *messenger*) has had modification. However, the Lord could reveal changes in the endowment if he wanted to, but so far he has only inspired changes in the method of teaching, perhaps to reflect our changing times and to take into consideration different local customs of a growing, worldwide Church. A living prophet in the LDS Church may be inspired by God to make changes, just as biblical prophets made changes. Some examples:

- God gave His people "an everlasting covenant" of circumcision (Gen. 17:8–10). Later the requirement was lifted (Acts 15).
- Paul taught that women should be silent and not teach (1 Corinthians 14:14–35). At other times women missionaries labored with Paul (Romans 16:1–4; Philippians 4;2–3; 1 Corinthians 11:5; Luke 2:36).
- When the children of Israel were incapable of living God's higher law, they received the lesser Mosaic law. During his earthly ministry, Christ again restored his higher law.
- God commanded David to build a temple (2 Sam 7:4:5). Later the Lord changed his original request because of David's serious sins and had Solomon construct the house of the Lord (1 Chronicles 28:6).
- Today, this idea of God modifying His commandments to meet circumstances is found in modern scripture: "I, the Lord, command and revoke, as

seemeth me good" (D&C 56:4). This was the case when entering into plural marriage was commanded in the Bible and revoked and later when commanded early in the LDS Church and revoked by the Lord in 1890.[30]

LDS Mason Greg Kearny also suggested that as the Saints became separated from Masons when they went west, the method of communication (the *messenger*) no longer needed to be connected to Masonry because almost all Latter-day Saints were no longer involved with that fraternal organization.

14. Since Latter-day Saints claim the LDS temple ceremony is biblical, what are some examples?

Frank Moore Cross, professor of ancient history, Harvard University, said, "I am both interested and delighted to see so much of ancient religious tradition, particularly Bible tradition, taken up into the religious structures and rituals of the Mormons."[31]

a) The word "temple" appears 191 times in the Bible. "house of the Lord" is used 213 times.

b) Malachi 3:1—Speaking of the last days, Malachi taught, "The Lord whom you seek will suddenly come to his temple."

c) Malachi 4:5—This verse states Elijah will precede Christ to "turn the hearts of the fathers to the children, and the hearts of the children to their fathers." (See also D&C 110 which records the fulfillment of this prophecy in the Kirtland Temple.)

d) Malachi 3:16—Speaks of a book of remembrance.

30. For a list of more of the Lord's changes in the Bible, see Scharffs, Gilbert W., *The The Missionary's Little Book of Answers*, [2002] p67 and 150.

31. Quoted in the LDS film *Between Heaven and Earth*, an excellent movie that contains several other statements by LDS and non-LDS leaders about the importance of temples.

e) 1 Corinthians 15:29—"Else what shall they do which are baptized for the dead, if the dead rise not at all? why are they then baptized for the dead?"

f) John 3:5—The absolute necessity of baptism and receiving the Holy Ghost for anyone of the human race to return to God's presence in heaven was given by the Savior when he said, "Except a man be born of water and of the Spirit, he cannot enter into the kingdom of God."

g) 1 Peter 3:19—"[Christ] went and preached to the spirits in prison."

h) 1 Peter 4:6—"For this cause was the gospel preached unto them which are dead, that they may be judged according to men in the flesh."

i) Nehemiah 7:5—When the Jews were freed from the Babylonian captivity and returned to Jerusalem and commanded to rebuild the temple Nehemiah said: "My God put into my heart that people should be recorded by genealogy . . . and I found a record of their genealogy.

j) The first three chapters of Genesis relating the creation story.

k) Genesis 9:12—God said, "This is a token of the covenant I have made between you and me."

l) Ex. 40:12-13—"And thou shall bring Aaron and his sons unto the door of the tabernacle of the congregation and wash them with water. And thou shalt put upon Aaron the holy garments and anoint him and sanctify him.

m) Psalms 23 starts, "The Lord is my shepherd, I shall not want" and ends, "Thou anointest my head with oil."

n) Num. 27:23—"Moses laid his hands upon Joshua."[32]

32. When Cecil B. DeMille was making the *Ten Commandments* he had

o). Isa. 40:31—Thou shalt run and not be weary, walk and not faint."

p) Isa. 2:2—"Thou shalt be called by a new name, which the mouth of the Lord shall name."

q) Revelation 3:12—Him that overcometh will I make a pillar in the temple of my God . . . . I will write upon him my new name."

r) Revelation 1:5—"[Christ] made us kings and priests unto God and his father."

s) Revelation 3:4-5—"Some have not defiled their garments and they shall walk with me in white, for they are worthy . . . . He that overcometh . . . I will confess his name before my father and before his angels."

t) 1 Kings 7:25—Solomon's Temple had a baptismal font that "stood upon [replicas of] twelve oxen."[33]

Latter-day Saints are often accused of not being biblical. The foregoing scriptures should help bring this charge to rest. In my study and teaching of Christian and non-Christian religions, I rarely find these scriptures taught or practiced today except by Jews, who still expect Elijah to come, and they set a meal for him at the Seder feast during Passover.

Jewish scholar Harold Bloom stated, "I will venture in this book, while Judaism and traditional Christianity are not biblical religions (despite their assertions) the American Religion

Moses conferring authority on Aaron by waving his hands in the air. When he asked David O. McKay if this was OK, the LDS Church president quoted this verse. In the film "laying of hands" is shown. The movie premiered in Salt Lake City.

33. In my World Religions classes, I always invited a Jewish professor from the University of Utah, Dr. Harris Lenowitz, to speak to my students. One day a member of the class asked, Do Jews baptize? His reply, "Who do you think Christians stole the idea from?" He went on to explain that today it is called a Mikva Bath and most synagogues have one. Converts to Judaism must have this ritual, the meaning of which, of course, is completely different from that in Christianity.

(Mormonism) is actually biblical, even when it exalts alternative texts" (Bloom,16).

Hundreds of other biblical scriptures could be quoted that only pertain to Mormonism. But this study is confined only to issues relating to temples. One more uniquely LDS temple concept is eternal marriage, covered next.

15. Since the Bible says there is no marriage in heaven, isn't marriage for time and eternity in the LDS temples a false concept?

The Bible does not teach that there is no marriage in heaven. Those who claim this like to quote Matthew 22:30, which states, "For in the resurrection they neither marry nor are given in marriage." Note that this verse does not say there are no married people in heaven. The verse is correct: there will be no marriages performed in heaven.

This life is the time to find a suitable mate and be married by officials who have been given this authority by today's living prophet to perform this marriage ceremony in an LDS temple. This ordinance is done for the living and by proxy for deceased ancestors and others. That is why Latter-day Saints do genealogical research to obtain the names of forefathers.

Marriage is ordained of God (D&C 49:15) and has been a religious ritual since the beginning of mankind. It does not make sense that if couples keep God's commandments, their loving family relationship would come to an end with "until death do you part" (not a biblical quote). Five verses, among others, strongly support this concept.

    a) Matt. 19:6—"What God has joined together, let not man put asunder."

    b) Eccl. 3:14—"Whatsoever God doeth, it shall be forever."

c) Genesis 2:18—"God said, it is not good that man should be alone."

d) Matt 18:18—Since Christ gave his apostles power and authority when he said to them, "Whatsoever thou shall bind on earth shall be bound in heaven," that would certainly include the Christian rite of marriage.

e) 1 Corinthians 11:11—"Neither is the man without the woman, neither is the woman without the man in the Lord."

Marriage and families for time and eternity are not part of Masonic ritual, or for that matter, of any other organization I know of.

All religions have some goal for afterlife. It is called by various names such as salvation, liberation, nirvana or mokska. This goal is always a personal quest. In teaching classes in World Religions, I found no religion, except Mormonism, that requires both a husband and a wife jointly to achieve the highest level of salvation in the next life.

Thanks be to the Lord for restoring, through the Prophet Joseph Smith, this comforting eternal truth, that can make marriage and family more beautiful and purposeful. It can soften the sting of death, when we know we will again rejoin the companionship of our loved ones in the next life.

16. Is there any support for LDS temple teachings being found in ancient civilizations?

Krister Stendahl, dean of divinity emeritus, Harvard University, and former head of the Lutheran Church in Denmark, said: "In antiquity . . . the Jerusalem Temple was a place where you went to carry out holy acts, sacrifices and the like. I feel that the Mormon experience of the Temple has sort of restored that meaning to the word Temple."[34]

Critics obviously do not want to look beyond Masonry as the source for the LDS endowment. In their efforts to discredit Mormonism, they are overlooking an abundance of old and new evidence.

We have given support from the Bible in questions 13 and 14, but many nonbiblical sources support the temple rituals restored through Joseph Smith. I think such discoveries are irrefutable and such sources were not known to the Prophet, as most were not discovered in his day.

If God established his Church with Adam and Eve, and numerous other ancient prophets through the ages, as LDS doctrine proclaims, it is to be expected that traces of sacred practices would be found throughout the world. These rites might have evolved into a different form, as was the case with Masonry. But if the same ritual appears in several groups, and they also are in the LDS ceremony, it is strong evidence that Joseph Smith (who did not know of the ancient practices) did restore through revelation from God an authentic temple endowment.

The *Encyclopedia of Mormonism* gives an overview of such sources: "Modified over the centuries these rituals existed in some form among ancient Egyptians, Coptic, Christians, Israelites, Masons, and in the Catholic and Protestant liturgies.

"Common elements include the wearing of special clothing, ritualistic speech, the dramatization of archetypical themes, instruction, and the use of symbolic gestures. . . . One theme common, of many, found in the Egyptian Book of the Dead, the Egyptian pyramid texts, and Coptic sources is 'prayer circles.'

"[Another theme] is man's journey through life and his quest, following death, to successfully pass the sentinels, guarding the entrance to eternal bliss with the gods. Though these

---

34. *Between Heaven and Earth* movie.

ceremonies vary greatly, significant common points raise the possibility of a common remote source" (Godfrey, Kenneth, "Freemasonry and the Temple," Godfrey, Kenneth W. *Encyclopedia of Mormonism,* Macmillan [1992] 2:528).

These ceremonies often include purification, special clothing, the Creation and the Adam and Eve garden story with the tree of life motif, coronation and admission to heavenly company. The *Encyclopedia of Mormonism* continues, "Like such ancient ceremonies, the LDS temple endowment presents aspects of these themes in figurative terms. It too presents, not a picture of immediate reality, but a model setting forth the pattern of human life on earth and the divine plan of which it is a part. Masonic ceremonies are also allegorical" (*Encyclopedia of Mormonism,* 2:528).

Other ancient records came to Joseph Smith "through the power of God," as the Prophet himself put it. These include the Book of Mormon and especially the Pearl of Great Price. This latter volume includes the book of Moses and the book of Abraham.

Another ancient source that supports the LDS temple rites is the Jewish Kabbalah. Critic Harold Bloom, a Jew, stated: "Researchers have not yet established to my satisfaction how much the Prophet Joseph knew about Jewish esoteric tradition, or Kabbalah. What is clear is that Smith and his apostles restated . . . the original Jewish religion." Bloom also said that he preferred the Judaism taught by the Kabbalah.[35]

Historian Richard Bushman agrees: "The Nauvoo Endowment is more akin to aspects of Kabbalah, the alternate native Jewish tradition that flourished for centuries alongside rational Judaism. As one commentator explains, Kabbalah's central impulse was a desire to encounter God.

"The Kabbalists sought not only to define and character-

---

35. Bloom, p 98

ize the Godhead . . . but to experience it.'" Bushman continues, "Joseph Smith's governing passion was to have his people experience God. To be sure, Joseph was not seeking a mystic God . . . , Joseph's God existed in time and space in a bodily form and cared for his children—all mankind".[36]

Man experiencing the true reality of deity is the main purpose of the LDS temple ceremony. And this theme permeates Joseph Smith's speeches and writings from the beginning of the Church. It also reflects what he learned in 1820, during the First Vision of the Father and Son, who appeared as separate beings—as they did to Stephen (Acts 7:55). Joseph wanted his followers and all the world to know the reality and personal nature of God the Father and his Son Jesus Christ, as he learned this knowledge for himself.Margaret Barker, a Methodist scholar in England and former president of the Society for Old Testament Study, spoke at the symposium on Joseph Smith at the Library of Congress. She agreed that Joseph Smith's ideas of a personal deity were reflected in the Old Testament. Her whole presentation was on how the Book of Mormon compared favorably with pre-Exile Judaism. In the Book of Mormon Lehi and his family left just before the exile that brought the Jews into Babylonian captivity. She also relied on alternate ancient texts such as the Dead Sea Scrolls to illustrate her points. It is remarkable, she said, how Joseph Smith knew all this.[37]

Barker could have tied these Old Testament–Book of Mormon pre-Exilic concepts of a personal God, in whose image we are literally created and who deals closely with his children, to the LDS temple, but she was, of course, unfamiliar with that ceremony (Gen. 1:26-27).

"Joseph Smith was an explorer, a discoverer and a revealer of past worlds," said Terryl L. Givens at the same Library of Congress symposium. His emphasis was similar to that of Mar-

36. Bushman, Richard, *Joseph Smith, Rough Stone Rolling* [2005]451
37. Welch, pp 69-82

garet Barker and also covered other areas of antiquity beyond the Old Testament. For example, Givens quoted from Augustine, who became the most influential Christian spokesman in the fourth century, after Christ. Augustine said, "What is now called Christian religion has existed among the ancients, and was not absent from the beginning of time."

Givens quoted the same idea from Jonathan Edwards, a famous Colonial American preacher who echoed the early Church Fathers, saying "that God had in fact imparted to several ancient people essential gospel truths that are subsequently lost." The idea of Jesus Christ's gospel going back to Genesis is lost to most of Christianity but not to Mormonism. Givens drew much of his presentation from the books of Moses and Abraham to illustrate Joseph Smith's knowledge of antiquity. Givens is distinguished professor of religion at the University of Virginia–Richmond.[38]

Although Mormonism and Masonry were not topics at the 2005 Washington, D.C., symposium, Latter-day Saints (who I estimate were about half the audience) heard presentations where voices from the past were quoted that tie in with the restored LDS temple ceremony. The non-LDS presenters did not realize how much they were validating Joseph Smith and the Temple endowment.[39]

17. Did Joseph Smith give the Masonic distress call just before he was murdered at Carthage?

It's true that Joseph Smith uttered the words, "Oh Lord my God" as he was being shot in the second story window at Carthage Jail. This is the first half of the Masonic distress call. The rest of the plea, "Is there no help for the widow's son?" was not given. If a Mason utters these words, any Mason hearing

38. Givens is familiar to Latter-day Saints as the author of *By the Hand of Mormon, The American Scripture that Launched a New World Religion.*
39. Welch, p 63-64

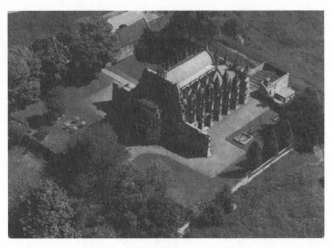

Rossyln Chapel near Edinburgh. It has many Masonic carvings and is the setting of the final scene in *The Da Vinci Code* book and movie. Location of one of the legends for the source of the Masonic distress call, "Is there no help for the widow's son?"

them must come to his rescue.

The origin of the distress call, some believe, originated with Hiram Abiff, the chief builder of Solomon's Temple. His mother was a widow when he was killed by other workers at the temple. Abiff refused to share ancient secrets with them, even though he gave the distress call.

Another source for the expression comes from the Rosslyn Chapel, near Edinburgh, the final scene in *The Da Vinci Code*. When we visited the chapel with its many Masonic carvings, the guide related to my wife and me another version of the source for the grand hailing of distress.

A master stonemason and his apprentice were each carving a column representative of Solomon's Temple. The teacher left for a time to study in Rome, and his student finished his own column based on a dream. When the teacher returned and saw how magnificent it was, he killed his student, who was the son

Carthage Jail. Scene of the murder of Joseph Smith as he allegedly gave the Masonic distress call.

of a widowed mother, as he gave the distress call.

Dan Brown apparently gave a coded message on the inside of the jacket of the *Da Vinci Code*, giving a hint of the subject of his next book. There are letters that are slightly bolder than the rest of the paragraph. The letters are:

ISTHERENOHELPFORTHEWIDOWSSON

There is a difference of opinion among historians. Some believe Joseph Smith intended to finish the distress call as a last-minute attempt to save his life. However, Joseph certainly knew there would be no friends in the mob with blackened faces, including Masons. The Nauvoo Masonic Lodge had been cut off by the Illinois Grand Lodge. Joseph certainly knew any friendly Masons in the crowd would be helpless against the mob. In the second or two that Joseph climbed out of the small window, it would have been impossible for him to raise both arms to the square, which is part of the distress call. I have never seen any claim that he did this.

Because his brother Hyrum was already dead and he knew the mob would not stop until they killed him, Joseph's only motive could have been to save the lives of the two apostles who were with him in the jail. Willard Richards and John Taylor, who was already severely wounded, both recorded Joseph only exclaiming, "Oh Lord, my God."

I believe the latter-day prophet was addressing the Lord Jesus Christ or God the Father, with whom he communicated during his life. Certainly they were close at hand. It seems possible that Joseph Smith, who had predicted his death, had last-minute anguish, as did the Savior, who in his final moments said, "My God, my God, Why hast thou forsaken me?" (Mark 15:34).

Joseph Smith had strong forebodings of his death. On April 7, 1829, a year before the Church was organized, the Lord had said, "Blessed are ye, for they can do no more unto you than they did unto me. And even if they do unto you even as they have done unto me, blessed are ye, for you shall dwell with me in glory" (D&C 6:29–30).

In March 1839, while still in Liberty Jail, the Prophet was told in a revelation, "Thy days are known, and thy years shall not be numbered less, therefore fear not what man can do, for God shall be with you forever and ever" (D&C 122:9).[40] There are several recorded prophecies Joseph Smith made about his life coming to an end. On August 6, 1842, he "declared to his brethren that he was not destined to go with them to the Rocky Mountains, yet they failed to grasp the meaning".[41]

In the spring of 1844, Orson Hyde of the Quorum of the Twelve Apostles recorded, "We were in council with Brother Joseph almost every day for weeks. Says Brother Joseph in one of those councils, 'There is something going to happen, I don't know what it is, but the Lord bids me to hasten and give you your endowment before the temple is finished.' He conducted us through every ordinance of the Holy Priesthood, and when

---

40. Smith, Joseph Fielding, *Essentials of Church History* [1950] 278
41. *Essentials,* 276

he had gone through with all of the ordinances, he rejoiced very much, and said, now if they kill me you have got all the keys and all the ordinances and you can confer them upon others, and the hosts of Satan will not be able to tear down the kingdom as fast as you are able to build it up".[42]

Probably one of highlights of Joseph's life was when he spoke at his last general conference in a grove in Nauvoo near the Temple. "This is the loveliest place and the best people on earth. Little do they realize the trouble that awaits them".[43]

In the days before Joseph Smith was murdered, he made several interesting statements. As hostile actions against the Saints intensified, Joseph and Hyrum felt if they left and started for the West, the threats against the Saints might let up. After they crossed the Mississippi, they learned that a posse arrived in Nauvoo and threatened to destroy the Saints if Joseph and Hyrum did not submit to arrest. Word also arrived that some of the Saints felt the Prophet had abandoned them. The prophet said, "If my life is of no value to my friends, it is of none to myself." Pondering the situation, Joseph Smith said to Hyrum, "If [we] go back . . . we shall be butchered." Joseph and Hyrum returned to Nauvoo to voluntarily submit to arrest.[44]

Before leaving Nauvoo, escorted by the posse from Carthage to stand trial, Joseph Smith said, "I told Stephen Markham that if I and Hyrum were taken again, we should be massacred, or I was not a prophet of God".[45]

As they left on horseback, Joseph Smith said, "I am going like a lamb to the slaughter, but I am calm as a summer morning. I have a conscience void of offense to God and all men. I SHALL YET DIE INNOCENT, AND IT WILL

42. *Church History in the Fulness of Times. Deseret Book.* [2000], 274.
43. *History of the Church,* 6:554
44. *Church History in the Fulness of Times,* 276
45. Berrett, 258

YET BE SAID OF ME--HE WAS MURDERED IN COLD BLOOD" (D&C 135:4; emphasis added).

Joseph Smith kept stopping and turning to look back, saying to the militia anxious to get him to Carthage, "If you had such a farm and knew you would not see it any more, you would want take to take a good look at it for the last time." In 2005, a large statue called *Joseph Smith's Last Ride* was erected across from the Nauvoo Temple depicting him and Hyrum's riding away on their horses.

Another prophecy was made during Joseph Smith's last night in jail. Several friends had volunteered to be with him. John Taylor, Willard Richards and Joseph's brother Hyrum were among those present. The prophet lay down on the floor next to Dan Jones, one of the first Welsh members of the LDS Church, Dan was converted while working in the United States as a riverboat captain. The previous May 11, he had been called to go to Wales on a mission and was preparing to go, but wanted to be with his Prophet.

Joseph Smith whispered and asked Dan Jones, "Are you afraid to die?"

Dan replied, "Has that time come, think you? Engaged in such a cause I do not think that death would have many terrors."

Joseph prophesied, "You will see Wales and fulfill the mission appointed to you before you die."[46]

The next morning the Prophet asked Dan to leave the jail and deliver a letter to Emma. He was also instructed by the Prophet to discuss their plight with Governor Thomas Ford, who was in Carthage at the time. Dan talked with Ford, informing him of a plot he had overheard to kill Joseph Smith. The governor told him not to worry and left for Nauvoo, even though he had

---

46. For a full account of the foregoing events, see Smith, Joseph Fielding, *Teachings of the Prophet Joseph Smith* [1976] 376-84.

promised Joseph Smith he would not leave without him.[47] The militia guarding the road to Nauvoo stopped Dan Jones. He tried to return to the jail, but the guards kept him away. Soon the Prophet and his brother were dead. Dan Jones lived to fulfill the prophecy and completed two remarkable missions to his homeland in Wales, baptizing some 1,000 converts.[48]

Another prophecy was yet to unfold. The massacre began when the mob rushed the jail. The guards assigned to protect the prisoners staged a mock defense and fired back with only blanks in their rifles. The assassins rushed up the stairs, shooting through the door, killing Hyrum and severely wounding John Taylor. Joseph Smith was shot twice from the doorway and twice while falling out of the window.

Willard Richards, who was only grazed by a bullet, expected to be killed at any moment, but those who came up the stairs retreated to the outside of the jail to fire more shots at the Prophet, if needed. Expecting the mob to return at any moment, Willard Richards heard the groans of the severely wounded John Taylor, who had crawled under a bed. Willard dragged him up to the third floor into the empty prison cell and covered him with an old mattress, so that he might live to tell the story.

The mob expected revenge, and when a voice was heard shouting, "The Mormons are coming!" they immediately fled Carthage. At that moment Willard Richards recalled words of

47. In 1994, at the sesquicentennial observance of Joseph Smith's death, President Gordon B. Hinckley, in a satellite broadcast from Carthage Jail, quoted from Illinois Governor Thomas Ford's *History of Illinois:* "Thus fell Joe Smith, the greatest imposter of all time."

48. Six months after the Prophet's death, in January 1845, Dan and his wife, Jane, went to Wales. When he arrived there were under 500 members, and when he left in 1849, the membership was 3,603. He completed a second mission to Wales, arriving in 1852. A year later there were over 5,000 members. The numbers would have been much higher, but many migrated to America during that time.

Joseph Smith years earlier, when the Prophet said, "Willard, the day will come when you will find yourself in the midst of balls of fire, but you will go unscathed."

These prophecies show that Joseph Smith knew that the time had come and his work on earth was finished. The kingdom of God was established for the last time, as ancient prophets had predicted. That is why I believe that when the Prophet said, just before being assassinated, "Oh Lord my God," he was addressing the Lord, awaiting entry into the eternal realm.

Conclusion

The most important question that needs to be answered is, "Was Joseph Smith a prophet of God"? When we come to know this through study and prayer, then our faith becomes unshakable.

John Taylor lived to record: "Joseph Smith, the Prophet and Seer of the Lord, has done more, save Jesus only, for the salvation of men in this world, than any other man that ever lived in it. In the short space of twenty years, he has brought forth the Book of Mormon which he translated by the gift and power of God; and was the means of publishing it on two continents; has sent the fullness of the everlasting gospel, which it contained, to the four quarters of the earth; has brought forth the revelations and commandments which compose this book of Doctrine and Covenants, and many other wise documents and instructions for the benefit of the men; gathered many thousands of the Latter-day Saints, founded a great city, left a fame and name that cannot be slain.

"He lived great, and he died great in the eyes of God and his people; like most of the Lord's anointed in ancient times, has sealed his mission and his works with his own blood, and so has his brother Hyrum. In life they were not divided, and in death they were not separated!" (D&C 135:3).

Appendix 1

A comment on the assassination and some statements made about Joseph Smith by non–Latter-day Saints in his day.

Critics sometimes consider a person's greatness a result of martyrdom. This has been said about Jesus Christ, Martin Luther King, Abraham Lincoln and others, as well as Joseph Smith. However, there were numerous persons assassinated throughout history that are long forgotten. These four are memorable not because they were martyred but because of their significant accomplishments and ideas.

In this study we have quoted several laudatory comments about Joseph Smith from non-LDS opinion makers in our day. Some memorable leaders did not get recognition until long after they were gone. When they were discovered, their adherents propelled them to greatness. Confucius is a prime example. Hardly anyone knew of him during his lifetime, but he left a lot of writings. Three hundred years after his death, Chinese society reached a low point with ever-increasing crime, corruption and endless wars. Something had to be done. Some leaders came across the writings of Confucius and liked them. "What do we have to lose? Let's try these ideas," they said. The ideas worked. Confucius is still a Chinese hero; decades of Communism could not eliminate his influence.

Joseph Smith did not have to wait for an assassination or centuries to be discovered. When he died at thirty-eight and one-half years of age, his followers numbered about 30,000. He succeeded against seemingly impossible odds, enduring endless persecution, yet his followers accepted him as a prophet of God. Although he had many enemies, he was admired and considered great not only by his own flock but by influential contemporary observers during his lifetime.

"This Joe Smith [must be] an extraordinary character. He is one of the great men of this age, and in future history will be ranked, with those who in one way or another, have stamped their impress strongly on society".[49]

"The Mormon movement is one of the most curious of the present age. It is inexplicable on the ordinary principles of philosophy. It is the beginning of a new dispensation or it is nothing. There can be no mistake in Joseph Smith. He is a master spirit and his ambition is to found a religious empire that will reach the uttermost ends of the earth. In Nauvoo and [vicinity] the Mormons number 10,000 souls, besides many cattle".[50]

Stephen Douglas: "If I could command the following of Joseph Smith, I would resign my seat in Congress and go to Oregon [and form a noble state], and if they would not receive us into the Union, we would have government of our own".[51]

---

49. *New York Times*, September 4, 1843
50. editorial in the *New York Herald*, November 18, 1841
51. Smith, John Henry, *An American Prophet*, 4. Once when Joseph Smith was dining with Judge Douglas at Carthage in 1843, the Prophet predicted that Stephen Douglas would be a successful politician in every office he ran for, unless he raised his voice against the Saints. Douglas won several elections, including defeating Abraham Lincoln for the United States Senate. On June 12, 1857, Douglas raised his voice against the Latter-day Saints at a speech in Springfield. In the presidential election of 1860 Douglas, a heavy favorite, lost to Lincoln in one of the biggest political upsets in United States history. A year later he was found dead in a small rented apartment in Chicago, apparently dying of loneliness and the effect of a crushing defeat. Earlier, in 1840, when the Latter-day Saints arrived in Illinois, both Lincoln and Douglas, serving in the state legislature in Springfield, had voted in favor of the Nauvoo Charter.

"Whether a liar or true man, it cannot be denied that Joseph Smith was one the most extraordinary persons of his time, a man of rude genius, who . . . will take his place among the notables of the world".[52]

One of the most influential men of the day, Josiah Quincy, mayor of Boston, came to Nauvoo and met with Joseph Smith. Years later in a speech in Philadelphia at a historical society meeting, he said: "It is not improbable that some future text-book, for the use of generations yet unborn will contain a [question] something like this: What historical American of the nineteenth century has exerted the most powerful influence on his countrymen? And it is by no means improbable that the answer to that [question] may thus be written: Joseph Smith, the Mormon prophet."

At the end of Josiah Quincy's visit with Joseph Smith, he said, "It seems to me, Mr. Smith, that you have too much power for any one man." Joseph replied: "In your hands or the hands of any other person, that might be true. But remember, Mr. Quincy, I am a prophet."[53]

52. Smucker, Samuel, *History of the Mormons* [1856] p 181-183
53. Quincy, Josiah, *Figures from the Past* [1883], 376, 397.

Appendix 2

A summary of why the LDS temple is vital and different from anything else on earth, and why I love to participate.

The following list shows that the temples of The Church of Jesus Christ of Latter-day Saints in our day are a unique and noble work, unlike anything found in Masonry or other organizations on earth.

1. The temple is a two-for-one bargain that helps individuals overcome selfishness.

Most problems that come up in life boil down to selfishness. We are more likely to overcome this tendency by making it a habit to go to the temple on a regular basis. We are able to renew our own commitments *and* at the same time perform the ordinances in behalf of distant relatives and others. To take time out of our busy schedules to do this work for those we have never met is an exercise in unselfishness that can carry over into our daily lives.

The Saints exercised unselfish sacrifice when in their days of poverty they built the Kirtland and Nauvoo temples. Latter-day Saints today unselfishly pay tithes that enable more temples to be built around the world.

2. The temple ceremony is an example that repetition is a vital principle of learning and communication skills.

Repetition is the key to learning. Taking a class in any subject is not enough to master the subject. Most of what we learn is forgotten unless we continue to focus and study what we want to remember. Hearing something once or twice, even a few times, may not be enough. When my wife asked me more than once to meet her at Third South and Second West at 3 p.m., I showed up at Second South and Third West at 3:30 p.m.

Telling our mate "I love you" on the honeymoon and just occasionally afterward would undermine our relationship sooner or later.

Is there any better way to renew our love for God than renewing our own covenants with him in the temple, especially when at the same time we are able to offer the blessing of eternal life to his other children who did not have the opportunity while living on the earth?

We cannot be reminded too often of eternal truths. The repetition of key concepts is a sound communication principle. By attending the temple often, not only do we go through the temple but the temple goes through us.

Participants often remark that each time they go to the temple they learn something new. As temple ordinance workers going to the temple twice a week, six hours at a time, my wife and I gained a greater appreciation for this sacred work.

3. The temple uses the same teaching method that the Savior used.

Facts and words are soon forgotten, but narrative is more easily remembered. The Savior used parables to teach higher principles to those prepared to understand. The temple ceremony is an allegory (a long parable) in which we are personally involved that spans mortal life and the eternities. Words, when they are part of a story, begin to make sense. Because of repetition the temple truths are engrained in our souls.

4 The house of the Lord answers the question that has concerned philosophers, theologians and all people throughout the ages.

Where did we come from? Why are we here? Where are we going? There are no more satisfying answers than those we receive in the temple.

5. The house of the Lord reminds us of our eternal heritage.

On one field trip to the Jewish synagogue with my World Religion class, the rabbi surprised us and invited us to witness a Jewish wedding. As he reminded the couple that they should always cherish their 4,000-year tradition, I felt gratitude in my own heart for being part of a 6,000-year earthly heritage, which actually began in a premortal existence.

6. Latter-day Saints are fulfilling prophecy when they attend the temple.

Malachi's prophecy that Elijah would precede the Lord's second coming and "turn the hearts of the fathers to the children and the hearts of the children to their fathers" is being fulfilled. The priesthood keys to this work for our forefathers was restored by Elijah to Joseph Smith and Oliver Cowdery in the Kirtland Temple on April 3, 1836 (D&C 110:13–15).

The late apostle LeGrand Richards and other LDS officials were visiting a synagogue in Jerusalem after dedicating the Orson Hyde Peace Park on the Mount of Olives. Elder Richards asked their host, the mayor of the Holy City, what the chair hanging from the ceiling meant. His reply: "That chair is for

Elijah when he returns to earth." Elder Richards said, "Oh, let me tell you about Elijah," and went into an LDS sermon for about an hour. The mayor responded graciously, tongue in cheek, "We might as well take down that chair."

Each time Latter-day Saints go to the temple they are performing the work of the Lord that was restored by Elijah.

7. Participation in the house of the Lord requires a high level of worthiness.

To be eligible to attend the temple, an LDS person is interviewed twice by authorized Church officials. Being able to answer the questions dealing with strict moral behavior brings personal satisfaction.

After I conducted one such face-to-face discussion with a woman, she said, "Thanks for giving me the opportunity to answer all those questions. It really makes me feel good."

8. The house of the Lord teaches us the principle of reporting our actions.

Where there is no reporting, there is little progress. In the temple we are reminded that reporting our activities is an eternal principle.

9. The temple emphasizes that we are responsible to the Lord for our behavior.

Some observers call this the "age of irresponsibility." We often hear excuses for bad conduct, such as heredity, being underprivileged, the environment, the media and the right to be free to do what we want.

President Dwight D. Eisenhower once wisely commented, "When we treasure our freedoms above our responsibilities, we soon lose our freedoms." Temple participation requires personal responsibility.

This belief in no way contradicts a belief that the grace of God is essential to our salvation. Latter-day Saints believe "it is by grace that we are saved, after all we can do" (2 Nephi 25:23). Some two dozen other Book of Mormon scriptures speak of the necessity of grace.

10. Continual, regular visits to the temple and renewing our covenants with the Lord give us strength to do more than just pay lip service.

It is easy for us to do as Paul warned: "The good that I would I do not; but the evil which I would not, that I do" (Rom. 7:19). Making frequent commitments to keep God's commandments is more likely to translate into doing something constructive with our lives.

11. In the house of the Lord the biblical teachings of the nature of God are emphasized.

"This is life eternal, that they might know thee the only true God *and Jesus Christ whom thou has sent*" (John 17:3; emphasis added). This is one of dozens of scriptures that emphasize the separateness of the Godhead, rarely believed in the world today, which is taught not only in the Bible but also the Book of Mormon and the LDS temples.

Other biblical examples: When Jesus was baptized, God spoke from heaven (Matt. 3:17). When Stephen was stoned, he saw a vision where Christ appeared on the right hand of God (Acts 7:55).

12. The temple emphasizes the true nature of man as the Bible teaches.

"And God said, Let us make man in our image, after our likeness. . . . So God created man in his own likeness, in the image of God created he them; male and female created he them" (Genesis 1:26-27). Numerous scriptures make this clear, as does the temple ceremony.

We know we are of God's kind, literally his children, not creatures, who lived in his presence before we were born. Latter-day Saints reject the common ex nihilo theory that God created man out of nothing. Paul taught, "We are the offspring of God" (Acts 17:29). Knowing of our divine nature brings dignity to our existence. This, too, is rarely taught anywhere.

13. The house of the Lord teaches the biblical principles of man's destiny.

When the Savior was being stoned for claiming to be the Son of God, he told his tormentors, "Is it not written in your law, I said, *Ye are gods*? (John 10:34; emphasis added). The Lord was referring to Psalm 82:6, which states, "Ye are gods; and all of you are children of the most High."

Other scriptures support this view. Peter taught, "Be partakers of the divine nature" (2 Peter 1:4). If we attain this biblical goal, we will continue to be our Heavenly Father's children and serve under his direction.

In a society where the degradation of man was (and is still) being proclaimed, humans defined in lowly terms, and Deity described as an abstract, impersonal concept, the heavens were opened and God and his Son Jesus Christ appeared to Joseph Smith and taught him the real nature of man.

14. Marriage that can last into the eternities is performed in the temple.

Knowing that our marriage can be extended into the next life can add a dimension of joy and stability to those who keep their temple covenants. Such unions have fewer divorces than civil marriages, and they can bring family solidarity.

When death comes to a mate or family member, the sting is less painful.

Most religions teach that any person can attain the goal of achieving a reward in the next life. In every religion I have taught, reaching this highest level is always a personal quest. Only in The Church of Jesus Christ of Latter day Saints can both a husband and wife together with their children reach this highest goal in eternity.

15. Qualifying for a temple marriage increases the chance of finding a wonderful mate.

If you and the person you to want marry both meet the strict standards that are required to have a temple marriage, you are basing your relationship on proven principles of success. Every one of the temple requirements, which are biblical principles, will strengthen a marriage. You can have peace of mind knowing that your mate has those same qualities that you do and that further a joyful and meaningful relationship.

16. A temple marriage promotes real love, because it is based on trust.

Church President David O. McKay taught, "It is more important to be trusted than to be loved." He obviously had in mind that real love without trust is impossible. When husband and wife promise before God to be true and faithful to each other, it is more likely they will keep their promises.

17. A meaningful love is more likely if both husband and wife are drawing closer to God.

Intimacy that is fulfilling and deeply loving is not just physical. When each marriage partner is drawing closer to God, each is drawing closer to the other. Going to the temple furthers this kind of relationship.

When Elder LeGrand Richards "proposed to Jane Ashton after his mission to the Netherlands, she ran from him, for his words were not what she wanted or expected to hear. 'There will always be one that will come ahead of you.' When he caught her, he had some explaining to do. 'I had such a wonderful experience in the mission field, I almost feel that I walked and talked with the Lord. My duty to him and his Church will have to come first. If you want second place, it is yours.' After his explanation, she wanted that place".[54]

When they were married, Sister Richards never had to worry about being second to another woman, a job or anything else.

18. The house of the Lord is a safeguard against the sin of adultery.

Hinduism, Buddhism, Confucianism, Jainism, Sikhism, Taoism, Zoroastrianism, Islam, Judaism and Christianity all teach chastity. But in practice, all too often, it does not happen.

Undoubtedly, a reason for so much immoral behavior in the world is that books, movies, television, magazines, the Internet, and popular heroes make immoral behavior seem attractive and acceptable. The media seldom portrays the diseases, abortions, unwanted children, broken homes, rape, murder and the costs to society that such behavior causes, let alone that it is breaking one of the Ten Commandments God (Exodus 20). In the temple we covenant to live the law of chastity.

19. The house of the Lord elevates women and men to their rightful positions as equally important in, but different, the eyes of God.

Although husbands and wives are equally important, they are different. When two people share a leadership role, whether

54. Tate, Lucile, *Legrand Richards, Beloved Apostle*

in business, government or marriage, confusion arises and often creates insurmountable problems.

Studies show that business partnerships fail much more often than sole proprietorships and corporations. Having two bosses is disastrous, as it is when there is no leader.

Some counselors dealing with problem children claim that if they only had a strong father in their lives their problems would go away. The temple ceremony reminds fathers and husbands not to abandon their role to lead in righteousness and love. Woman's role is not one of subjugation, and a wife needs not support a husband who is abusive and not righteous.

The temple ceremonies are designed to help men and women reach their full potential. Both men and women receive the same priesthood blessings in the temple. The husband, however, makes temple covenants that remind him to be the spiritual leader to his family, something most righteous women want. Once when trying to be a matchmaker in a singles ward, I suggested to my Relief Society president that she be more friendly to a certain man whom I thought would be ideal for her. Her answer was very revealing about how women feel. "Oh, he's a really nice guy, but I need someone who would be a strong leader in our home."

20. Temple-attending parents have the power of example in raising children.

Paul taught us to be an example of a believer. The prominent Christian missionary Dr. Albert Schweitzer, said there are three ways to train children properly: Example, example and example.

21. The house of the Lord gives us a time and a place to meditate.

With our busy schedules, meditation time is hard to find. It should be part of prayer and worship. Too often my prayers are like pushing a doorbell and running away. The Lord said, "Be still and know that I am God" (Psalm 46:10).

22. Going to the temple fulfills our need to have sacred ritual in our lives.

Ritual has been part of God's people throughout the Bible and was part of ancient temple worship. In some churches in our day, ritual has taken on a public display involving pomp and ceremony. Sometimes churches use ritual for the forgiveness of sins. Still others emphasize that faith is all that is needed. Most non-Christian churches stress works.

The Latter-day Saint perspective combines all three: faith in Christ, good works and temple ritual. The LDS sequence for these three elements requires faith in Christ and good works (righteous living) to precede sacred temple ordinances.

23. Temple participation enables us to become more like Christ the Savior.

Jesus Christ our Savior and Redeemer, on behalf of all mankind, overcame death and brought about resurrection and immortality through his ordeal in Gethsemane and on the cross. "For as in Adam all men die, even so in Christ shall all be made alive" (1 Corinthians 15:22).

The Savior not only overcame death but gave teachings and ordinances that go beyond immortality to provide *eternal life*. Two essential practices for this level of resurrection are baptism and receiving the gift of the Holy Ghost. Christ made this clear,: "Except a man be born of water and of the Spirit, he cannot enter into the kingdom of God" (John 3:5).

The vast majority of mankind have had no opportunity during their lifetime to receive these and other ordinances necessary to return to God's presence. They are taught the gospel in the spirit world under the direction of the Savior. Peter referred to Christ's visit to those spirits (1 Pet. 3:19) and continued, "For this cause was the gospel preached also to them that are dead, that they might be judged according to men in the flesh" (1 Pet. 4:6).

Paul also spoke of essential ordinances for all God's children who die without having received baptism. "Else what shall they do which are baptized for the dead, if the dead rise not at all? Why are they then baptized for the dead?" (1 Corinthians 15:29). He referred to this practice as evidence of the resurrection. Nonbiblical documents also show that baptisms in behalf of the dead were once practiced. The biblical practice of baptisms in our day in behalf of the dead is unique to LDS temples.

Thus we see that a sinless Christ overcame death in behalf of the inhabitants of the world, doing what they could not do for themselves. Latter-day Saints are striving to be Christlike by performing the essential ordinances, such as baptism and marriages, in behalf of those children of God who have died without being able to do these ordinances themselves.

24. Work in temples on behalf of the dead in temples encourages us to pursue family history.

Latter-day Saints are motivated to do genealogical research to find the names of their ancestors. This itself is a rewarding quest. This effort also creates a desire to write the history of these forefathers. All this family history becomes a book of remembrance for each family member.

Once, when I became angry with one of our daughters, she went to her room sobbing. After a while I went to apologize for my harsh words. The door was slightly ajar and inside was silence. I was deeply moved when I saw her sitting on her bed going through her personal book of remembrance, which included photos of our family over the years.

At a family home evening we discussed what to do in case of a fire. One child asked, "Can we take anything with us?" I replied, "No, we just get out as quickly as possible." Our youngest son said, "I'll at least grab my book of remembrance."

One of the first words he spoke as a toddler, tugging at my wife's skirt and pointing to the shelf with the book of remembrance, was "book, book!" Time and again he wanted to sit on her lap and have her turn the pages, as she told the story behind each picture.

Sometimes our kids took their books to school for "show and tell." Another son went away to an eastern university. After a few months he requested us to send him his book of remembrance to show to his friends.

These books also include vital information of all our known ancestors and the dates the saving ordinances were performed in the temple.

25. Performing ordinances for our own ancestors in the house of the Lord brings extra joy.

The temple experience is extra meaningful when we go to the house of the Lord in behalf of our own forefathers. Once my aging mother arranged for family members to perform temple ordinances for the latest ancestors she had researched. Afterwards we had dinner at a local restaurant. We were all enjoying a good time with much laughter. My mother sat in silence. One of us asked, "What's wrong Mom?

After a pause she quietly replied, "I was just wondering how wonderful Great Grandma and Great Grandpa Barth must feel right now, after all these years, being together again with their family."

We witnessed the spirit of Elijah in action.

26. The house of the Lord is available to everyone who chooses to qualify.

In our world there is only one Heisman Trophy winner each year. Just one best actor and one best actress Oscar awards are given. Not everyone gets to be a millionaire. Only a few get Nobel prizes. Some clubs don't admit women. It takes a small fortune to join some organizations. Other groups and professions require educational degrees unattainable by most people.

In God's kingdom anyone can participate in temple ceremonies, whether a bank president or welfare recipient, sitting side by side, dressed the same, in white. All it takes is membership in The Church of Jesus Christ of Latter-day Saints and qualifying for a temple recommend, which is based on commitment to righteous principles. There are no "No Vacancy" signs.

27. The temple may be the only place in the world where strict observance of biblical commandments are required to enter.

If there is any other organization that requires biblical principles of righteousness for participation, I'm not aware of it.

28. The temple ceremony gives the correct meaning of the term "chosen people."

Many groups throughout history and today claim to be God's favored people. This is often based on birth, race, nationality, or religion. Much hate and many wars were and are still perpetuated by the way this concept has changed from the way the Lord intended.

Latter-day Saints claim to be Christ's official Church, as the name indicates. This causes some to think Mormons believe they are God's chosen people, but critics do not understand that to Latter-day Saints "chosen" requires a person to choose to follow the Lord. It means it is something that is earned. And earning it is not based on birth, nationality, race, social position, wealth, or belonging to a certain religion.

This interpretation is reflected somewhat in the words of Abraham Lincoln: "I'm not so concerned whether God is on my side, but that I'm on God's side." God loves all his children. the Book of Mormon teaches, "The Lord esteemeth all flesh in one; he that is righteous is favored by God" (1 Nephi 17:35). We, not God, determine who is favored.

This is also made clear in the Book of Mormon where the Prophet Zenos' allegory of the tame and wild olive trees is quoted by Jacob. This is a portrayal of the world, past and future. It relates how the Lord kept working with the house of Israel, represented by the tame olive tree. Time after time God tried to work with his people as the Bible teaches, but wickedness prevailed. He grafted wild branches into the tree (the Gentiles), but again the tree became corrupt.

At the end of the world, the allegory teaches, "As many as will not harden their hearts will be saved in the kingdom of God. Wherefore, my beloved brethren, I beseech you in words of soberness that you would repent and come with full purpose of heart and cleave unto God, as he cleaves unto you. And while his arm of mercy is extended towards you in the light of day, harden not your hearts" (Jacob 6:3-7).

29. The house of the Lord gives credence to the LDS claim of being God's official church on earth because it makes it possible for all mankind to return to God's presence.

Qualifying to live during the Millennium, however, is no guarantee of eternal life with God. Every religion claims to be the only, or the best, path to reach the highest eternal goal. Most churches and religions claim a person needs to adhere to the beliefs of their organization to be eligible to obtain this exalted goal. But would God's official Church be a private club?

I have found no other church that has a program that reaches out to every one of God's children, giving them the option to choose eternal life with our Eternal Father, and which unites families and has meaning and purpose, except The Church of Jesus Christ of Latter-Saints.

This is not only manifest by one of the largest, if not the largest, volunteer missionary efforts of any church in the world, but by building temples around the globe, at a record pace, where this saving opportunity is extended.

These are some of the reasons I witness and testify that The Church of Jesus Christ of Latter-day Saints is building God's kingdom on the earth and why I love to go to the temple.

Joseph Smith described this work: "Now, what do we hear in the gospel which we have received: A voice of gladness! A voice of mercy from heaven; and a voice of truth out of the earth; glad tidings for the dead; a voice of gladness for the living and the dead; glad tidings of great joy. . . . Behold thy God reigneth! . . . Shall we not go forward in so great a cause?" (D&C 128:19, 22).

Appendix 3

When the LDS Church reached 100 years in 1930, there were seven operating temples. In 1955, the number was nine with the dedication of the Bern, Switzerland temple, the first outside the USA and Canada. As a missionary at the time, I remember hearing Brigham Young quoted. On June 22,1856, twenty years before there was a single operating temple in the Chuch, he said: "To accomplish this work there will . . . be thousands of temples" (JD 3:372).

With 124 temples at the end of 2006, and ten more under construction or announced, Brigham Young's statement does not seem impossible. There were 77 new temples completed since President Gordon B. Hinckley became president in 1995. President Hinckley has dedicated 85 temples, 63 as president of the Church.

In one of his darkest hours in Liberty Jail, Joseph Smith said, "How long can rolling waters remain impure? What power shall stay the heavens? As well might man stretch forth his puny arm to stop the Missouri River in its course, or to turn it up stream, as to hinder the Almighty from pouring down knowledge from heaven upon the heads of the the Latter-day Saints" (D&C 121:33). The following is a list of current temples, the year they were dedicated, and who dedicated them.

1. St. George Utah, 1877, Daniel H. Wells

2. Logan Utah, May 1884, John Taylor
3. Manti Utah, May 1888, Lorenzo Snow
4. Salt Lake, April 1893, Wilford Woodruff
5. Laie Hawaii, 1919, Heber J. Grant
6. Cardston Alberta, 1923, Heber J. Grant
7. Mesa Arizona, 1927, Heber J. Grant
8. Idaho Falls Idaho, 1945, George Albert Smith
9. Bern Switzerland, 1955, David O. McKay
10. Los Angeles California, 1956, David O. McKay
11. Hamilton New Zealand, 1958, David O. McKay
12. London England, 1958, David O. McKay
13. Oakland California, 1964, David O. McKay
14. Ogden Utah, 1972, Joseph Fielding Smith
15. Provo Utah, 1972, Harold B. Lee (reader)
16. Washington D.C., 1974, Spencer W. Kimball
17. Sao Paulo Brazil, 1978, Spencer W. Kimball
18. Tokyo Japan, 1980, Spencer W. Kimball
19. Seattle Washington, 1980, Spencer W. Kimball
20. Jordan River Utah, 1981, Marion G. Romney
21. Atlanta Georgia, 1983, Gordon B. Hinckley
22. Apia Samoa, 1983, Gordon B. Hinckley
23. Nuku'alofa Tonga, 1983, Gordon B. Hinckley
24. Santiago Chile, 1983, Gordon B. Hinckley
25. Papeete Tahiti, 1983, Gordon B. Hinckley
26. Mexico City Mexico, 1983, Gordon B. Hinckley
27. Boise Idaho, 1984, Gordon B. Hinckley
28. Sydney Australia, 1984, Gordon B. Hinckley
29. Manila Philippines, 1984, Gordon B. Hinckley
30. Dallas Texas, 1984, Gordon B. Hinckley
31. Taipei Taiwan, 1984, Gordon B. Hinckley
32. Guatemala City Guatemala, 1984, Gordon B. Hinckley
33. Freiberg Germany, 1985, Gordon B. Hinckley
34. Stockholm Sweden, 1985, Gordon B. Hinckley

35. Chicago Illinois, 1985, Gordon B. Hinckley
36. Johannesburg South Africa, 1985, Gordon B. Hinckley
37. Seoul Korea, 1985, Gordon B. Hinckley
38. Lima Peru, 1986, Gordon B. Hinckley
39. Buenos Aires Argentina, 1986, Thomas S. Monson
40. Denver Colorado, 1986, Ezra Taft Benson
41. Frankfurt Germany, 1987, Ezra Taft Benson
42. Portland Oregon, 1989, Gordon B. Hinckley
43. Las Vegas Nevada, 1989, Gordon B. Hinckley
44. Toronto Ontario, 1990, Gordon B. Hinckley
45. San Diego California, 1993, Gordon B. Hinckley
46. Orlando Florida, 1994, Howard W. Hunter
47. Bountiful Utah, 1995, Howard W. Hunter
48. Hong Kong China, 1996, Gordon B. Hinckley
49. Mount Timpanogos Utah, 1996, Gordon B. Hinckley
50. St. Louis Missouri, 1997, Gordon B. Hinckley
51. Vernal Utah, 1997, Gordon B. Hinckley
52. Preston England, 1998, Gordon B. Hinckley
53. Monticello Utah, 1998, Gordon B. Hinckley
54. Anchorage Alaska, 1999, Gordon B. Hinckley
55. Colonia Juarez Chihuahua Mexico, 1999, Gordon B. Hinckley
56. Madrid Spain, 1999, Gordon B. Hinckley
57. Bogota Colombia, 1999, Gordon B. Hinckley
58. Guayaquil Ecuador, 1999, Gordon B. Hinckley
59. Spokane Washington, 1999, Gordon B. Hinckley
60. Columbus Ohio, 1999, Gordon B. Hinckley
61. Bismarck North Dakota, 1999, Gordon B. Hinckley
62. Columbia South Carolina, 1999, Gordon B. Hinckley
63. Detroit Michigan, 1999, Gordon B. Hinckley
64. Halifax Nova Scotia, 1999, Gordon B. Hinckley
65. Regina Saskatchewan, 1999, Boyd K. Packer
66. Billings Montana, 1999, Gordon B. Hinckley
67. Edmonton Alberta, 1999, Gordon B. Hinckley

68. Raleigh North Carolina, 1999, Gordon B. Hinckley
69. St. Paul Minnesota, 2000, Gordon B. Hinckley
70. Kona Hawaii, 2000, Gordon B. Hinckley
71. Ciudad Juarez Mexico, 2000, Gordon B. Hinckley
72. Hermosillo Sonora Mexico, 2000, Gordon B. Hinckley
73. Albuquerque New Mexico, 2000, Gordon B. Hinckley
74. Oaxaca Mexico, 2000, James E. Faust
75. Tuxtla Gutierrez Mexico, 2000, James E. Faust
76. Louisville Kentucky, 2000, Thomas S. Monson
77. Palmyra New York, 2000, Gordon B. Hinckley
78. Fresno California, 2000, Gordon B. Hinckley
79. Medford Oregon, 2000, James E. Faust
80. Memphis Tennessee, 2000, James E. Faust
81. Reno Nevada, 2000, Thomas S. Monson
82. Cochabamba Bolivia, 2000, Gordon B. Hinckley
83. Tampico Mexico, 2000, Thomas S. Monson
84. Nashville Tennessee, 2000, James E. Faust
85. Villahermosa Mexico, 2000, Thomas S. Monson
86. Montreal Quebec, 2000, Gordon B. Hinckley
87. San Jose Costa Rica, 2000, James E. Faust
88. Fukuoka Japan, 2000, Gordon B. Hinckley
89. Adelaide Australia, 2000, Gordon B. Hinckley
90. Melbourne Australia, 2000, Gordon B. Hinckley
91. Suva Fiji, 2000, Gordon B. Hinckley
92. Merida Mexico, 2000, Thomas S. Monson
93. Veracruz Mexico, 2000, Thomas S. Monson
94. Baton Rouge Louisiana, 2000, Gordon B. Hinckley
95. Oklahoma City Oklahoma, 2000, James E. Faust
96. Caracas Venezuela, 2000, Gordon B. Hinckley
97. Houston Texas, 2000, Gordon B. Hinckley
98. Birmingham Alabama, 2000, Gordon B. Hinckley
99. Santo Domingo Dominican Republic, 2000, Gordon B. Hinckley
100. Boston Massachusetts, 2000, Gordon B. Hinckley

101. Recife Brazil, 2000, Gordon B. Hinckley
102. Porto Alegre Brazil, 2000, Gordon B. Hinckley
103. Montevideo Uruguay, 2001, Gordon B. Hinckley
104. Winter Quarters Nebraska, 2001, Gordon B. Hinckley
105. Guadalajara Mexico, 2001, Gordon B. Hinckley
106. Perth Australia, 2001, Gordon B. Hinckley
107. Columbia River Washington, 2001, Gordon B. Hinckley
108. Snowflake Arizona, 2002, Gordon B. Hinckley
109. Lubbock Texas, 2002, Gordon B. Hinckley
110. Monterrey Mexico, 2002, Gordon B. Hinckley
111. Campinas Brazil, 2002, Gordon B. Hinckley
112. Asuncion Paraguay, 2002, Gordon B. Hinckley
113. Nauvoo Illinois, 2002, Gordon B. Hinckley
114. Hague Netherlands, 2002, Gordon B. Hinckley
115. Brisbane Australia, 2003, Gordon B. Hinckley
116. Redlands California, 2003, Gordon B. Hinckley
117. Accra Ghana, 2004, Gordon B. Hinckley
118. Copenhagen Denmark, 2004, Gordon B. Hinckley
119. Manhattan New York, 2004, Gordon B. Hinckley
120. San Antonio Texas, 2005, Gordon B. Hinckley
121. Aba Nigeria, 2005, Gordon B. Hinckley
122. Newport Beach California, 2005, Gordon B. Hinckley
123. Sacramento California, 2006, Gordon B. Hinckley
124. Helsinki Finland, 2006, Gordon B. Hinckley

Bibliography

Bloom, Harold. *The American Religion*. New York, 1992.

Bushman, Richard. *Joseph Smith, Rough Stone Rolling*. 2005.

Church History in the Fulness of Times. Salt Lake City, 2000.

Godfrey, Kenneth W. "Freemasonry and the Temple." *Encyclopaedia of Mormonism*. Edited by Daniel H. Ludlow. New York, 1992.

——— "Causes of Mormon/Non-Mormon Conflict in Hancock County." Ph.D. dissertation. BYU, 1967.

Griffith, Michael T. *A Ready Reply: Answering Challenging Questions about the Gospel*. 1994.

Haag, Michael and Veronica. *The Rough Guide to The Da Vinci Code*. London, 2004.

Hickenbotham, Michael W. *Answering Challenging Mormon Questions*. 1995.

Hogan, Mervin B. "Mormonism and Freemasonry: The Illinois Episode." In *Little Masonic Library*. Ed. Silas H. Shepherd, Lionel Vibert, and Roscoe Pound. 5 Vols. Richmond, Va., 1977.

Ivins, Anthony W. *The Relationship of "Mormonism" and Freemasonry*. Salt Lake City, 1934.

Leonard, Glen M. *Nauvoo: A Place of Peace, a People of Promise*. Salt Lake City and Provo, 2002.

McGavin, E. Cecil. *Mormonism and Masonry.* Salt Lake City, 1954.

Madsen, Truman G., ed. *The Temple in Antiquity.* Provo, Utah, 1984.

Nibley, Hugh W. *The Message of the Joseph Smith Papyri: An Egyptian Endowment.* Salt Lake City, 1975.

Oaks, Dallin H., and Marvin Hill. *Carthage Conspiracy.* Chicago, 1975.

Packer, Boyd K. *The Holy Temple.* Salt Lake City, 1980.

Pick, L. and G. Norman Knight, *The Pocket History of Freemasonry.* Rev. ed. London, 1977.

Shepherd, Silas H., Lionel Vibert, and Roscoe Pound, eds. *Little Masonic Library.* 5 vols. Richmond, Va., 1977.

Scharffs, Gilbert W., *The Truth about "The God Makers."* Salt Lake City, 1988.

——— *The The Missionary's Little Book of Answers.* Salt Lake City, 2002.

Shugarts, David A. *Secrets of the Widow's Son.* 2005.

Smith, Joseph. *History of The Church of Jesus Christ of Latter-day Saints.* 2d ed, rev. Edited by B.H. Roberts Salt Lake City, 1932–51. 7 vols. 1902-12.

Smith, Joseph Fielding. *Answers to Gospel Questions.* 5 vols. Salt Lake City, 1957–66.

——— *Essentials in Church History.* 18th ed. 1963.

Welch, John W. "The Worlds of Joseph Smith." *BYU Studies.* 44, 4 (2005).

Whitney, Orson F. The *Life of Heber C. Kimball.* Salt Lake City, 1992.

Winwood, Richard I. *Take Heed That Ye Be Not Deceived.* 1995.

Author's Biographical Information

Gilbert W. Scharffs received a bachelor of arts degree in marketing from the University of Utah, a master's degree in business from New York University, and a Ph.D. in history of religion and the Bible and modern scripture from Brigham Young University.

Dr. Scharffs taught religion classes in the educational system of The Church of Jesus Christ of Latter-day Saints in seminary, and for 27 years at the Salt Lake Institute of Religion adjacent to the University of Utah, where he also served as director for a number of years and taught classes in scripture, Church History, and World Religions. He also taught classes for BYU in Provo, Salt Lake, and recently Nauvoo.

He is the author of *Mormonism in Germany, 101 Reasons I Like to Go to Church, The Truth about the Godmakers, The Missionary's Little Book of Answers,* and several articles in Church publications.

Brother Scharffs' Church callings have included missionary in Germany, bishop (twice), member of a stake presidency, and member of a Church writing committee. He and his first wife, Virginia (deceased) are the parents of Yvette, Brett, Lisa, and Calvin.

In 2001 Brother Scharffs married Judy Short, who had previously taught and coached in the Granite and Jordan school districts. Together they served as ordinance workers in the Salt Lake Temple. They currently serve as Public Affairs missionaries in the Europe West Area, with headquarters in London.